Throwing Fire

Projectile Technology Through History

In *Throwing Fire,* historian Alfred W. Crosby looks at hard, accurate throwing and the manipulation of fire as unique human capabilities. Humans began throwing rocks in prehistory and then progressed to javelins, atlatls, and bows and arrows. We learned to make fire by friction and used it to cook, drive game, burn out rivals, and alter landscapes to our liking. Our exploitation of these two capabilities figured in the extinction of many species, and may have played a role in the demise of Neanderthals. In historic times we invented catapults, trebuchets, and such flammable liquids as Greek Fire, a napalm-like substance that stuck to whatever it hit and could not be extinguished with water. About 1,000 years ago we invented gunpowder, which led to guns and rockets, enabling us to literally throw fire. Gunpowder weaponry accelerated the rise of empires and the advance of European imperialism. In the twentieth century gunpowder weaponry enabled us to achieve unprecedented mayhem – the most destructive wars of all time. This trend peaked at the end of World War II with the V-2 and atomic bomb, at which point species suicide became possible. Faced with possible extinction should we experience World War III, we have turned our projectile talents to space travel. Throwing fire, which might make Earth uninhabitable for humans, may make it possible for our species to migrate to other bodies of our solar system and even other star systems.

Alfred W. Crosby is Professor Emeritus in American Studies, History and Geography at the University of Texas at Austin. His previous books include *Ecological Imperialism: The Biological Expansion of Europe, 900–1900* (Cambridge, 1986) and *The Measure of Reality: Quantification and Western Society, 1250–1600* (Cambridge, 1997), which was chosen by the *Los Angeles Times* as one of the 100 most important books of 1997.

Throwing Fire

Projectile Technology Through History

ALFRED W. CROSBY
University of Texas at Austin

CAMBRIDGE
UNIVERSITY PRESS

CAMBRIDGE UNIVERSITY PRESS
Cambridge, New York, Melbourne, Madrid, Cape Town, Singapore,
São Paulo, Delhi, Dubai, Tokyo, Mexico City

Cambridge University Press
32 Avenue of the Americas, New York, NY 10013-2473, USA

www.cambridge.org
Information on this title: www.cambridge.org/9780521156318

First published 2002
Reprinted 2009
First paperback edition 2010

Printed in the United States of America

A catalog record for this publication is available from the British Library.

Library of Congress Cataloging in Publication Data

Crosby, Alfred W.
Throwing fire : projectile technology through history / Alfred W. Crosby.
p. cm.
Includes bibliographical references and index.
ISBN 0-521-79158-8
1. Projectiles – History. I. Title.
UF750 .C76 2002
623.4'51 – dc21   2001052556

ISBN 978-0-521-79158-8 Hardback
ISBN 978-0-521-15631-8 Paperback

To Allegra and Xander

I shot an arrow into the air,
It fell to earth I knew not where...

Henry Wadsworth Longfellow,
"The Arrow and Song"[1]

Every moving thing that liveth shall be meat for you.

Genesis, 9:3

...Believe me, the stars
will fit your pockets.

Bruce Boston, "Interstellar Tract"[2]

---

[1] "The Arrow and the Song," *The Poems of Henry Wadsworth Longfellow,* ed. Louis Untermeyer (New York: Heritage Press, 1943), 140.

[2] *Technology in American Literature,* eds. Kathleen N. Monahan and James S. Nolan (Lanham, NY: University Press of America, 2000), 264.

Contents

Preface

In early 2001 I finished writing this book about mankind's penchant for, and skill with, projectiles and combustion, and the resulting effects on life on this planet. I wrote this book because I think that historians too often focus on the finest grained and most subtle evidence, and often, after great effort, produce studies so finely grained and subtle as to be quite nearly unintelligible.

I decided to begin with the gross and undeniable fact that humans and, probably, other hominid species effected change at a distance via projectile and fire, and were alone in doing so. We have, by pursuing a love affair with this capability, altered the course of our history and of evolution on earth, and have ventured into space.

One of the manifestations of this capability that intrigued me most was the power it gave us to produce effects out of all proportion to means. A Clovis hunter spears the last mammoth in North America; a Zionist fanatic shoots Yitzhak Rabin; Wernher von Braun hits London with a rocket and later helps send rockets to the moon; and Osama bin Laden dispatches lieutenants to hijack airplanes and on September 11 of 2001 murders thousands in New York City and Washington, D.C.

We are fascinated with explosive projectiles, an obsession that benignly manifests itself in firework displays at holidays, weddings, and other such events; in Mehemed II's giant bombard; in the Vengeance Weapons; and in the atomic bomb of World War II. We are obsessed with delivering projectiles that produce at a distance loud noises and fireballs. John Milton knew that when he created an alluring Satan and made him a Pre-Adamite inventor of gunpowder and cannon "whose roar Embowell'd with outrageous noise the Air, And all her entrails tore, disgorging foul Their devilish, chain'd Thunderbolts and Hail...."[1]

I should have left my copy of *Paradise Lost* on the shelf and waited for the terrorist attacks of September 11 to use for my illustrative example. Osama bin Laden – charismatic and murderous – makes a worthy stand-in for Milton's Satan, although he was forced to substitute fanaticism for expertise and to parasitize on the technology of enemies in order to procure and direct his projectiles. The effects fell short of Milton's Satanic artillery, but impressed all of us. The Twin Towers stood "as Rocks, but down they fell" and " Angel on Arch-Angel roll'd...."[2]

The heaving of projectiles characterizes our species as unequivocally as bipedal locomotion and tool making. On the fateful September 11, 2001, the Mars Odyssey Mission vehicle, launched by rocket in April to determine the content of Mars' surface and to detect water and therefore the possibility of life there, past or present, was approaching that planet at a speed, relative to the Sun, of 24 kilometers a second. On October 24th, as American missiles fell on Afghanistan, the vehicle started into orbit around the fourth planet from the Sun and began its inspection.[3]

Whether we end in the pit or space, we will do so while throwing fire.

---

[1] John Milton, *Paradise Lost, Paradise Regained, and Samson Agonistes* (Garden City, N.Y.: International Collectors Library, 1969), 148.

[2] Milton, *Paradise Lost,* 148.

[3] http://www.jpl.nasa.gov/releases/2001/release_2001_186.html

Who, Why, and How

Don't you think it's right to rake up the past?
I don't feel that I know what you mean by raking it up.
How can we get at it unless we dig a little? The present
has such a rough way of treading it down.

> Henry James, "The Aspern Papers"[1]

Only the past is present...

> W. H. Auden, "At The Grave of Henry James"[2]

We humans are impressed with our superiority: the author of
the eighth psalm ranks us "but a little lower than the angels." And
so we are shocked to learn that we share about 98.5 percent of

---

[1] *The Great Short Novels of Henry James,* ed. Philip Rahv (New York: Dial
Press, 1944), 528.
[2] W. H. Auden, *Selected Poems,* ed. Edward Mendelson (New York: Vintage
Books, 1979), 120.

our DNA with chimpanzees.[3] That other percent and a half must be quite something because chimps exist in only remnant populations while there are six billion of us. We venture nearly everywhere, including under the sea and in orbit around our planet. We dispatch rockets to explore the solar system and beyond. And we plan to visit Mars. I doubt that any dog, even if its IQ were multiplied by a thousand, would want to do anything as pointless in terms of creature comforts as that.

To deal with the mystery of our success we need to trace the trajectory of our species and family in its full length. As writers and readers we are merely 5,000 years old. The first heroes of the written medium, Gilgamesh, Abraham, and so on, are like early movie stars – Douglas Fairbanks and Errol Flynn, for instance – that is, they are latter-day celebrities. As a species we are at the very least twenty times older than the first cuneiform tablets. As a genus, the taxonomic unit that includes ours and closely related species (of which there were many in the past and none now), we are enormously older than that.

It is disconcerting to think of Egypt's pyramids as recent, like the hippies' long hair, but any accurate timeline of hominid or even *Homo sapiens* history would cram both together at the extreme near end. To understand ourselves we must begin to think not in terms of centuries or even millennia but of megablocks of millennia. We are Stone Age creatures, lately arrived in a world that is, ironically, both alien and of our making.

An investigation of a history that includes the full stretch of our separate lineage will oblige us to accept as evidence bones, flints, and inferences based on relic features and propensities of

[3] Jared Diamond, *The Third Chimpanzee: The Evolution and Future of the Human Animal* (New York: HarperCollins, 1993), 23.

our present-day bodies and mentalities. Opportunities for mistakes proliferate, but refusal to try would leave us locked in the narrow confines of recorded history like an amnesiac railroad traveler trying to find out who he is, where he has been, and where he is going by scanning the newspaper left on the seat beside him. That is a good place to start, but he should also examine the contents of his pockets and go to the rear car and look back down the track.

If we want to know about human beings, we have to begin by defining them. What is distinctive and what is unique about being human? We are highly intelligent, but perhaps that is not as definitively important as we are inclined to think it is. Otherwise, why has that trait only appeared once in all of evolution? Flying, one of natural selection's tours de force, has appeared at least three times. Anyway, intelligence was not what got us our start: the brains of the Australopithecines, the earliest hominids, were only a third as big as ours.[4]

Of our several identifying characteristics – our infinitively expressive speech, our system of sexual intercourse by choice rather than by glandularly dictated rutting season,[5] our devotion to tool making, and so on – I have picked only three. I will begin with a brief survey of bipedalism, necessary because bipedalism evolved very early among our ancestors and may have been the most decisive of all our evolutionary changes as we veered off to become a genetic category all by ourselves. Explanation of what makes our genus what it was and is must include what the literati might call *explication de pied*.

---

[4] *The Cambridge Encyclopedia of Human Evolution,* eds. Steve Jones, Robert Martin, and David Philbeam (Cambridge: Cambridge University Press, 1992), 116–17.

[5] Diamond, *Third Chimpanzee,* 77.

Second, let us investigate what may be the least publicized of our distinctive capabilities: we are the planet's best throwers. All of us, male and female, from eight year olds to dodderers, can throw further and more accurately than members of any other species. Today this capability is of vanishing significance for our survival, but remains an obsession anyway, continuing on in our most popular games, most of which are ballistic. These include both world and American football, basketball, baseball, cricket, golf, hockey, tennis, Ping-Pong, jai alai, and in our species-wide effort to hit the wastebasket across the room from the desk with crumbled paper balls. It lives on in our efforts to blast in cans off fences and to fire rockets at Mars. We are unique in our delight in effecting change at distances, at three yards, at a hundred million miles.

Third, we must consider our manipulation of fire. We are unique among all creatures in routinely utilizing fire. Many animals communicate by oral signals, which might, at a very long stretch, be called speech. Chimpanzees and several other species are clever enough to use simple tools. Apes throw after a fashion. But only we habitually make fire, which we have been doing for so long that one might speculate that it may have a genetic component by now. We put candles on birthday cakes and altars, we ignite fireworks to celebrate – we love fire.

The description of *Homo sapiens* as consisting of two-legged throwers who start fires is as impeccably precise and exclusive as a definition of our species as the one that today detonates hydrogen bombs and dispatches telescopes into orbit.

Evidence pertaining to the evolution of bipedalism and the other traits to be considered is hard to come by. The most reliable kind is the actual stuff – bones, flints, bits of charcoal, and their locations vis-à-vis each other and surroundings – that has survived from the deep past of our lineage, but there is not a lot of it per 100,000 years, so to speak. Paleoarcheologists spend much of their careers in remote regions, chancing malaria and bandit attacks, to collect the stuff, then years in front of computer screens to interpret these materials. There they perform prodigies of insightful analysis (and sometimes remind even friends that blood squeezed from a stone is usually that of the squeezer).

Another useful kind of material evidence is our own selves, our bodies and minds, which are the estate and effects bequeathed to us by our ancestors. We are mostly what we are in physique, physiology, and mentalité because of what they were and experienced. To cite obvious examples, our brains are big because they were useful to our ancestors and our little toes are little because they were not. To cite a less obvious case, consider the location of our larynx, low in our throats as compared to other animals', which has the disadvantage of making it possible for us "to swallow the wrong way." The compensatory advantage is that the larynx in that position plays an essential role in speaking. Ipso facto, speech has been worth the risk of choking to death, that is, it has been very important for many generations to *Homo sapiens* survival.[6]

Lastly, we can, albeit very gingerly, turn to analogy: that is, if recent humans acted in such-and-such a way, then ancient hominids may have done the same. If, for instance, the likes of Captain Ahab and Queequeg killed whales, huge and immensely dangerous, with spears propelled by hand, then it is plausible to think that humans may have done the same with mammoths many thousands of years ago.

---

[6] Philip Lieberman, *The Biology and Evolution of Language* (Cambridge: Harvard University Press, 1984), 271–328.

Physicists and chemists can offer laboratory proofs. Paleoanthropologists and historians, like geologists, can only try for plausibility. We who are students of deep time must turn cartwheels on top of the parapet and yell defiance at the sharpshooting critics. This is useful because if either the acrobat proves to be right or the snipers to be accurate, we learn something.

ONE

The Pliocene: Something New Is Afoot

> That's one small step for a man, one giant leap for mankind.
>
> Neil Armstrong (1969)

We start with the Australopithecines,[1] the earliest hominids, that is, the earliest creatures clearly our relatives and not shared with chimpanzees. If we inquire into what was most like us about them, millions of years ago, we may discover what is most ancient in hominid heritage and perhaps what is the true essence of humanity. Were they bright – like us? (a question best asked while preening before a computer screen). No, their brains were only about a third the size of ours.

We make tools – spoons, forks, internal combustion engines, atomic energy plants – and expect our ancestors to have made

---

[1] I should point out that I will eschew whenever possible numerical dates, even those that allow for pluses and minuses of hundreds of thousands of years, and, with few exceptions, I will omit hominid species names as well. I don't want to pose as a paleoanthropologist nor do I want to become the innocent bystander so often injured in the combat of experts. I am interested in the chronological sequence of our ancestors and in their physical and mental capabilities, not dates or geneologies per se. I have my own fish to fry.

tools. Did Australopithecines make anything we recognize as even the crudest of tools, for instance, a chipped cobble with sharpish edges?[2] No, they didn't. They no doubt made use of rocks and branches at hand, which they may have modified slightly for the purpose, for instance, stripping bark from twigs to extract termites from logs. Chimps do that sort of thing, but have never elaborated on such behavior. Australopithecines or the species in hominid evolution that followed obviously did, but not to begin with.[3]

There is one feature of the Australopithecine skeleton that even a weekend paleontologist can spot immediately as prefiguring his or her own skeleton. It is the foot, which Dr. Frederic Wood, author of the classic *Structure and Function as Seen in the Foot,* celebrates as conferring "upon Man his only real distinction and provide his only valid claim to human status."[4]

The foot began as a hand, and its twenty-six bones – seven tarsals, five metatarsals, fourteen phalanges – are obviously versions of the bones of the hand: the thumb as the big toe, the four fingers as the other toes, the heel of the hand as the heel of the foot. The palm has lengthened into an arch, the toes have undergone abbreviation. The big toe has swiveled into line with the other toes and lost its vaunted opposability, and can no more reach the little toe than the stars.

The foot began as a hand, an organ of many capabilities, an organ for manipulation (a word derived from the Latin for hand). Making a foot of it would seem to be a case of making a sow's ear

[2] Bernard Wood, "The Oldest Whodunnit in the World," *Nature,* Vol. 385 (January 23, 1997), 292; Shanti Menon, "Hominid Hardware," *Discover,* Vol. 33 (May 1997), 34.

[3] Readers who want to sample the debates about who was and who was not ancestral to *Homo sapiens* should read David S. Strait, Frederick E. Grine, and Marc A, Moniz, "A Reappraisal of Early Hominid Phylogeny," *Journal of Human Evolution,* Vol. 32 (January 1997), 17–82.

[4] Frederic Wood, *Structure and Function as Seen in the Foot* (London: Bailliere, Tindall and Co., 1944), 2.

out of a silk purse. The sacrifice of function involved proclaims that the advantages in becoming bipedal (for that is what we are dealing with here) must have been immense.

The foot's job is to bear our weight and to get us around in this world. What a deflation, you may think, of its raison d'etre since its glory days as a hand. That, however, is like saying that a hammer is inferior to a Swiss Army knife because the former has one talent and the latter many. But the hammer can do one important thing much, much better than the Helvetian multipurpose jackknife. It can hammer.

The foot's function of bearing weight requires stability, but it must not be so solid as to transfer every shock with the ground to the delicate structure of the body above. The foot's function of providing locomotion involves thrusting down and back, that is, elasticity, but of course it must not be so elastic as to entail instability.

Take your choice: the foot is either a brilliant compromise fulfilling these contradictory requirements or a jerry-built improvisation put together with the parts available.

The outside of the foot, the part in contact with the ground that runs from the ball of the foot around to the heel, is a static supportive organ. But we do not stump through the world: the toes and the arch from the ball behind the big toe back to the heel are elastic, mobile, and dynamic and provide propulsion. The longitudinal arch and the less obvious transverse arch between the inside to outside of the foot absorb the shocks that flesh (certainly the foot) is heir to.[5]

The foot is only one part of what we need to move about while upright. Above it is the ankle, a joint that experiences the shock of the foot's contact with the ground and must be supple enough to swivel forward and back, left and right, in order to accommodate to variations in that surface and the shifts, to and fro, side to side, of the weight above it. The knees likewise suffer pounding and also

5 Wood, *Structure*, 247, 259, 261.

swivel forward and back (but not otherwise, if all is well). The hip joints also get pounded and must allow for rotation of the leg as well as its swing forward and back. In between the hip and the knee the thigh bone, the femur, tilts inward from the former joint to the latter. We are all skeletally knock-kneed. Otherwise we would waddle. Try walking with your feet exactly under the hip joint. Awkward. Widen the placement of your feet only a bit more and you will have the gait of a movie monster.

There are also our shoulders and arms, swiveling and swinging in opposition to the movement of our legs. They supplement our knock-kneed femurs in damping the sway from side to side. There is our back, arranged not in an arch, the architecturally sturdy form favored by other quadrupeds, including apes, but in an S-curve, the bottom half curving in and the top half out. We thus have managed to retain a central column with which to brace a torso and also to stand up straight (if you won't quibble about calling S a straight line) and to twist and sway whichever way is needed from moment to moment. Backaches and displaced disks are the price.

And, on top of the flexible neck, which is on top of everything else, is the head, that boulder whose misdirected mass can send the whole assemblage veering off in unexpected directions.

Myriad bundles of muscles connect and surround the hard bones. The exquisitely sequenced and coordinated contractions and relaxations of these soft tissues enable us to move like good animals rather than bad machines. Imagine the human body as a stick figure with each major flexible boney connection – two ankles, knees, hips, shoulders, elbows, one back, one neck – capable of only five positions each. How many positions is this simplified version of ourselves capable of assuming? That would be five times five eleven times over. The final total is 488,281,125. The total if calculated on the full range of the body's possible postures would be – literally – beyond calculation.

It is the functions of our muscles (and the nerves that direct them and transmit their return messages) that we find so difficult to reproduce in robots and why it is so much easier to produce one that rolls than one that walks on two or even four feet. The lurch of the movie's Frankenstein (any able-bodied child could thumb his or her nose and skip away from that monstrosity) is about as good as our engineers have managed with walking machines.[6]

Let us consider the miracle of getting around on two feet. We will ignore running, which involves having both feet off the ground part of the time. Let us consider unspectacular walking, the merest example of which turns out to be more complicated neuromuscularly than a Beethoven symphony is musically. Walking is the process of leaning forward to fall on your face and then interrupting that mistake by stepping forward – and then proceeding on with the next mistake and the next interruption for as long as it takes to get where you want to go. When you catch your toe on a curb the interruption is delayed and you complete your sprawl.

Walking, the linear movement of the body forward, involves the shifting of the weight from one base, the left foot, let us say, to the right and then back. To avoid sprawl, the body's center of gravity must shift back and forth, keeping up with and above the supporting foot. That could be accomplished by placing each foot with each step directly in line with the other foot's last placement, which would have us walking as if on a tightwire, about to topple laterally, and would require considerable expenditure of energy to swing each foot around the other with every step.

We compromise. The advancing foot lands ahead of the other with its inside edge close to or on the inside edge of a line drawn directly forward of the other foot, which at the moment is supporting the body's weight. All this involves a wagging about of

6 J. Furusho and A. Sano, "Development of Biped Robot" in *Adaptability of Human Gait: Implications for the Control of Locomotion*, ed. Aftab E. Patla (Amsterdam: Elsevier Science Publishers, 1991), 301.

practically everything, feet, legs, hips, shoulders, arms, in whatever direction is required to keep the whole on an even keel.[7]

If we had observed an Australopithecine proceeding across the
landscape of Ethiopia some three and a half million years old, we
would have seen that it walked more like a modern human than a
chimpanzee. The bones of its arms, pelvis, and knee joint indicate
that. Even better evidence of that gait turned up in 1976 in
Tanzania: the footprints of three individuals as they walked across
a moist layer of volcanic ash one day long, long ago.

These individuals walked on two feet. There are no indications
of knuckle-dragging whatsoever. The print of each step lies just off
the line of the previous step. The mark of the big toe (the former
thumb) is about twice as big as that of the toe next to it, like ours,
and the spacing between the toes no greater than between those of
people today who usually go barefoot or of even many habitual
wearers of shoes. The big toe print is parallel with the others. On
each stride the heel clearly struck the ground first, then the body
weight rolled forward along the outside of the arch to the outside
of the ball and then across to the ball to the big toe. Then the toes
and forefoot thrust back against the ash for the stride forward,
pushing up a bit of the ash back against the ball.

These footprints would not attract our attention if found in
the sand of a beach today.[8] The stride that made them was, like
ours, a pas de deux for one person's two feet more complicated
than any ever choreographed for two dancers.

---

[7] Marion Broer, *Efficiency of Human Movement*, 3rd ed. (Philadelphia: W. B.
Saunders Co., 1973), 145, 151, 153.

[8] *Laetoli, A pliocene Site in Northern Tanzania*, eds. M. D. Leakey and J. M.
Harris (Oxford: Oxford University Press, 1987), 498, 500; R. H. Crompton
et al., "The Mechanical Effectiveness of Erect and Bent-hip, Bent-Knee'
Bipedal Walking in *Australopithecus afaransis*," *Journal of Human
Evolution*, Vol. 35 (July 1998), 71; Richard L. Hay and M. D. Leakey, "The
Fossil Footprints of Laetoli," *Scientific American*, Vol. 246 (February 1982),
51. For another interpretation, see Ian Tattersall and Jeffrey Schwartz,
Extinct Humans (New York: Neuramont Publishing Co., 2000), 95.

I know of only a single appreciation in literature of that peculiar gait, and it is worth pausing for. Aldous Huxley described it in his flapper-generation novel, *Antic Hay,* with gentle recognition that sometimes the survival of the species may require momentary inattention to firm footing in favor of sexual signaling. His heroine, Myra Viveash,

> crossed the dirty street, placing her feet with a meticulous precision one after the other in the same straight line, as though she were treading a knife edge between goodness only knew what invisible gulfs. Floating she seemed to go, with a little spring at every step and the skirt of her summery dress – white it was with a florid pattern printed in black all over it – blowing airely out around her swaying march.[9]

The Australopithecines' feet were no doubt better for climbing than Myra Viveash's, and they probably fled to the trees when lions prowled and may have spent their nights there, but, like Myra, clearly they had rejected two hands good for a thousand purposes and turned them into feet at least as good, perhaps better, for locomotion on the level than for climbing trees. The Australopithecines were on their way down to the ground where their teeth and claws (mere fingernails!) were inferior to those of rivals and enemies, where these bipeds were easy to tip over and couldn't run as fast or jump as far as any of the large or even medium-sized predators.

It would seem that our ancient relatives went to enormous trouble to move from a desirable neighborhood to a very dangerous one. But sometimes the new kid on the block works up a new set of tricks. He has to. As Darwin put it a century and a quarter ago, it may "have been an immense advantage to man to have sprung from some comparatively weak creature."[10]

---

9 Aldous Huxley, *Antic Hay* (New York: The Modern Library, 1923), 98.
10 Charles Darwin, *The Origin of Species by Means of Natural Selection and The Descent of Man and Selection in Relation to Sex* (New York: The Modern Library, n.d.), 443.

The First Acceleration: Hominids Become a Keystone Species and Their Own Worst Enemies

The ability to throw, to commit violence at a distance with rock, spear, javelin, dart, and arrow, transformed hominids from prey to predator and made them the first creatures of size who could effect change at a distance. That equipped them to survive and exploit even the largest land animals. They made a comparable accession of power when they learned to manipulate fire.

Then humans (we can start using that term instead of hominids) had their first population explosion and, to minimize competition for food, avoided each others' presence, in time migrating to lands where there were no others like them. There they fully exercised the conqueror's privilege.

When this migration of mutual repulsion reached its geographical ultimates, humans, again of necessity, reversed their age-old propensity of dividing into small groups. They became farmers and pastoralists, coalesced into villages and cities, multiplied again, only this time cheek to jowl, progressed from raids to war, and became each others' worst enemies. They achieved advances in projectile technology that must still impress us.

TWO

The Pliocene and Pleistocene: "You Are What You Throw"[1]

To man He gave the ability to think and the hand.

Ibn Khaldun (c. 1377)[2]

One can hardly doubt, that a man-like animal who possessed a hand and arm sufficiently perfect to throw a stone with precision, or to form a flint into a rude tool, could, with sufficient practice, as far as mechanical skill alone is concerned, make almost anything which a civilized man can make.

Charles Darwin (1871)[3]

*B*irds shifted their weight and the responsibility for surface locomotion to their hind legs to free their forelimbs for flight. Hominids

[1] Robin Dennell, "The World's Oldest Spears," *Nature,* Vol. 385 (February 27, 1997), 768.
[2] Ibn Khaldun, *The Mugaddimah: An Introduction to History,* trans. Franz Rosenthal, ed. N. J. Dawood (Princeton, NJ: Princeton University Press, 1989), 46.
[3] Charles Darwin, *The Origin of Species and The Descent of Man* (New York: The Modern Libtary, n.d.), 432–3.

sacrificed hind hands for feet so as to stand up and free their forelimbs to take up an infinity of duties, opening up the possibility that their descendents might, a few million years of vicissitudes later, become us. The trade-off has obviously been to our advantage, but there are substantial disadvantages. Bipedal locomotion is more like walking on stilts than, for instance, a wolf's easy lope. How many four-footed animals of size can you outrun? How many times have you ever seen a four-footed creature fall over? How many times have you tumbled from your bipedal altitude? Bipedalism, declares Owen Lovejoy, prominent physical anthropologist, "is a lousy way of getting around."[4]

We may have traded two of our four hands for feet and committed ourselves to life spent largely on the ground because several million years ago climate change reduced African forest and replaced it with a mosaic of trees and grassland, that is, because we couldn't make a living if we remained exclusively in or among the trees.[5] But one wonders whether a halfway measure, the knuckle-walking of the apes, might not have served us better than full bipedality.[6] Chimps can lope about pretty well on hind hands and forehand knuckles and in times of danger can almost certainly scurry up into the trees faster than Australopithecines ever could (even though the latters' feet surely were more prehensile than ours). The chimps' compromise between four- and two-handedness would seem to have

---

[4] Richard Leakey and Roger Lewin, *Origins Reconsidered* (New York: Doubleday, 1992), 81, 87.

[5] James Shreeve, "Sunset on the Savanna," *Discovery*, Vol. 17 (July 1996), 116–25.

[6] We aren't even sure when knuckle-walking appeared or who did the knuckle-walking. See Henry Gee, "Palaeontology: Return to the Planet of the Apes," *Nature*, Vol. 412 (July 12, 2001), 131–2. We are not descendents of all the species of Australopithecines, but I don't want to get involved in the debates of which were and were not our ancestors. Therefore, I resort to vague references to the latter.

been better adapted for surviving in a woodland-grassland mosaic than an incautious commitment to bipedality.

But bipedality paid off. So much so that the wrists of the Australopithecines from whom we probably are descendents lost the sculpting of the small wrist bones that had enabled them to lock together to firmly take the weight of the upper body, that is, to knuckle-walk efficiently. That alteration may have left the Australopithecines a bit wobbly, but with a now flexible wrist with new capabilities.[7] Among them may have been the final whipsnap necessary for completing a hard throw and also helpful for knocking off a useful flake from a stone core.

Let us assess what physical structures and faculties the Australopithecines inherited from their upstairs ancestors that were markedly different from what groundlings commonly possessed and that became, in new adaptations, particularly those involved in throwing, useful to these downstairs apes. They inherited a brain that depended more on visual, compared to olfactory, information than is common among animals. In the trees the visual sense is especially valuable because it provides instant information about matters of immediate importance – the branch to reach for when tumbling off a perch, to cite an obvious example. With this brain came an uncommon awareness of the full geometry of surroundings, an advantage enhanced by the location of the eyes on the front of the head, eyes with overlapping fields of vision. These creatures had, thereby, excellent depth perception, important for tree traveling and available for unprecedented functions on the ground below – like judging exactly how far away a target is.

---

7 Brian G. Richmond, "Evidence that Humans Evolved from a Knuckle-walking Ancestor," *Nature*, Vol. 404 (March 23, 2000), 382–5; Personal communications from Brian G. Richmond. See also Mike Dainton, "Paleoanthopology: Did Our Ancestors Knuckle-walk?" *Nature*, Vol. 410 (2001), 324–5.

They had, like their ape relatives, upper limb structures (collarbones and ball-and-socket shoulders) that enabled them to revolve their arms in full circles. Elephants can do that with their trunks and octopi with their tentacles, but only primates can do it with limbs stiffened with bones. They can sit in a tree with one hand at the end of its 360-degree rotating arm grasping a branch above or below or to the front or to the back while the other holds a fruit or scratches a nose or bum. They can throw overhand pretty well if they want to.

This shoulder had enabled the Australopithecines' ancestors to travel nimbly through the trees. Apes, too big and heavy to run along branches like squirrels, usually travel along one branch while holding on to another, or they swing along while hanging on to a branch from below or from one branch to another branch: they brachiate.

At the far, the distal, end of the Australopithecines' remarkable arms was the stunningly versatile primate hand, quite like our own, "the narrowest hinge" of which, according to Walt Whitman, "puts to scorn all machinery."[8] The Australopithecine's thumb, nearly as opposable to the fingers and full palm as ours, was powerful and yet dexterous, capable of instantly cooperating with the fingers in any of a number of kinds of grips, including, in all probability, the three-jawed chuck grip favored by baseball pitchers. The hand terminated not in claws, but in soft, sensitive fingertips for molding and clinging to a variety of surfaces, like those of missiles of wood, bone, and stone.[9]

Wonderful – upstairs – but how would these forelimbs, now freed from bearing weight, promote the Australopithecine as a

[8] Walt Whitman, *Complete Poetry and Collected Prose* (New York: The Library of America, 1982), 57.

[9] Frank R. Wilson, *The Hand: How Its Use Shapes the Brain, Language, and Human Culture* (New York: Pantheon Books, 1998), 19–20, 28, 29; Colin Tudge, *The Time Before History* (New York: Touchstone, 1997), 169.

good bet for survival? Owen Lovejoy speculates that they enabled their bipedal owner to carry things,[10] which made transporting and sharing food possible, encouraging family and band loyalty, and made toting children easier as well, which enormously increased the odds of their surviving. (Just yesterday in the grocery store I marveled at the versatility of our own down-to-earth arboreal forelimbs as I observed a mother hold a squirming baby in one arm and hand while managing with the other her car keys and a pen with which she was signing a chit.)

The experts used to speculate that an early and the most important advantage of bipedality, which released the forehands for new tasks, must have been the ability to make tools, weapons specifically. We have, however, no evidence of tool making – that is, no tools *made of stone* – for hundreds and hundreds of thousands of years after the Australopithecines' appearance. Of course, they may have made very simple tools of perishable materials like wood, but if they were markedly better than chimps at making tools, wouldn't at least some of them have been stone, of which we would have found some examples?

Perhaps they did use stone. Perhaps their innovation was not in how they altered the material, but in the use they made of it. They may have thrown rocks. It was one of the very few things hominids could do better than other animals. Archer fish spit with admirable accuracy, but not far. Chimpanzees throw sticks and stones, but only for short distances, sometimes with intention but inaccurately, and usually underhand.[11] Maybe the Australopithecines' decisive innovation was that they usually threw to hit things and, with aim, as well as velocity, enhanced by their flexible wrists, often did.

---

[10] Leakey and Lewin, *Origins Reconsidered* (New York: Doubleday, 1992), 81, 87.

[11] Jane van Lawick-Goodall, *In the Shadow of Man* (Boston: Houghton Mifflin Co., 1971), 53, 114, 116, 118, 123, 210; Andrew Whiten and Christophe Boesch, "The Culture of Chimpanzees," *Scientific American*, Vol. 284 (January 2001), 65.

The resulting advantage may have been razor thin, but decisive. For example, the female Australopithecine with a newborn, faced with a carnivore, no longer had only impossible choices, that is, to fight, to try to flee burdened with her child, or to desert her offspring and run off alone. Now she might, at least sometimes, discourage the attacker with a cascade of rocks and sticks. As William Calvin, physiologist and speculator on the origins of projectile technology, opines, "The first star pitcher may have been a mother."[12]

New species do not pop up like jack-in-the-boxes, not even by the standards of the proponents of punctuated equilibrium. Sometimes, though, decisive change can be relatively swift if a given organ or genetically rooted behavior does not alter in form so much as it does in purpose: swords into plowshares, so to speak, or vice versa.

One of the more freakish occurrences in the course of evolution was our distant ancestors' discovery of the suitability for throwing of their arboreally evolved hand, arm, shoulder, and body. The movement of the ape body brachiating in dipping arcs forward and under and past one arm–hand gripping a branch and forward and under and past the other evolved into the movement of throwing, a metamorphosis as wonderful as that of dinosaur feathers, probably evolved for warmth or display, becoming bird feathers for flight.

Hominids turned brachiation upside down. The hand, which had been fixed (if only for a moment) to the branch to support the body swinging below, now became the traveler. Now it was the body that remained stable, relative to the hand and its arm. In overhand throwing the shoulder functioned as in brachiating (i.e., as a pivot), but now in order to deliver a missile, not the body.

---

[12] William Calvin, "Did Throwing Stones Shape Hominid Brain Evolution?" *Ethology and Sociobiology*, Vol. 3 (1982), 119–20.

✳ ✳ ✳

Recorded history is replete with proofs of the importance of ballistics. The examples of the Old Testament's David and our Lee Harvey Oswald dispatching, respectively, Goliath and President Kennedy come to mind. But recorded history goes back only a paltry few thousand years. What actual evidence do we have that throwing was important long ago, possibly millions of years ago?

The best we have and can possibly have is ourselves. As I already said, we, in our physiques and faculties, are the products of what the past has done to our species and genus. Our bodies are lockboxes of our ancestors' experience.

Consider the delivery of a baseball pitcher, which is somewhat different from that of a javelin thrower or a cricket bowler, but will serve our purpose. Almost 50 percent of the velocity of a baseball thrown hard is contributed by the legs and torso. At one instant the lower mass of the ensemble lunges in the direction of the throw while the arm and hand reach back. Then the lower mass halts so as to enhance the snap forward of the limb and hand.[13] The act of throwing is balletic before it achieves the ballistic.

Presiding over all this cascade of flexing and relaxing, of modulated lunging and reeling, is the neurophysiological system, ticking down through the list of necessary actions – first this and then that and this until finally the fingers release the missile during an instant too tiny for me to appreciate except quantitatively. (I am, like you, better equipped to perform the act than to understand how I do it.)

In order to throw a missile and hit a target the size of a rabbit at four meters, I must release the missile within a duration, "a launch window," of *eleven milliseconds*. That act, which most of us can perform some of the time and some of us all the time, is in

---

[13] For a full description of this act, see Wilson, *The Hand*, 323–4. Also see Marion Broer, *Efficiency of Human Movement*, 3rd ed. (Philadelphia: W. B. Saunders Co., 1973), 235, 241.

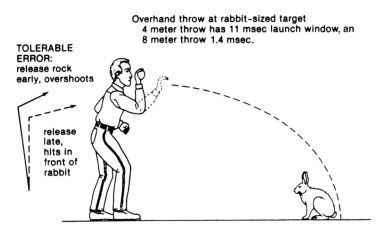

Overhand throw at rabbit-sized target
4 meter throw has 11 msec launch window, an
8 meter throw 1.4 msec.

TOLERABLE
ERROR:
release rock
early, overshoots

release
late,
hits in
front of
rabbit

Figure 1. The launch window for an overhand throw at a rabbit-sized target is eleven milliseconds at a distance of four meters and 1.4 milliseconds at a distance of eight meters. William H. Calvin, "The Unitary Hypothesis" in Gibson and Ingold, eds. *Tools, Language and Cognition in Human Evolution* (Cambridge: Cambridge University Press, 1993).

the same category of natural miracles as a bat's ability to snatch insects out of the dark guided by ecolocation. If the rabbit is eight meters away, the window is only 1.4 milliseconds (Fig. 1).[14] And what would the window be if the target happens to be a bounding gazelle at a dozen meters?

Capabilities, once in the genes, are available for duties other than those that first engendered them there. Throwing accurately is a matter of the intricate sequencing and timing of multitudes of neural firings, of the marshaling of myriads of cells to act and react in accordance with an orchestration of millions of synaptic

[14] William H. Calvin, "The Unitary Hypothesis: A Common Neural Circuitry for Novel Manipulations, Language, Plan-ahead, and Throwing?" in *Tools, Language and Cognition in Human Evolution,* eds. Kathleen R. Gibson and Tim Ingold (Cambridge: Cambridge University Press, 1993), 240, 234, 246–7. A version of this for the lay reader can be found in Calvin's *The Cerebral Symphony: Seashore Reflections on the Structure of Consciousness* (New York: Bantam Book, 1990).

impulses. Surely nature would not have been so prodigal as to waste such a grand capability on only one task?

The neurophysiologist Calvin proposes that the meticulous avalanche of neural events necessary for hard and accurate throwing served as a "scaffolding" for other multitudinously sequential behaviors – the playing and enjoyment of music, for example. Another, he suggests, is what may be humanity's most important capability: language.[15] Such speculations wait on research that will, for instance, tell us which areas of the brain "light up" when we aim and throw. Are they the same as those that do so when we speak?

The human brain as considered by Calvin is a glorious computer for processing Niagaras of signals, but he does not concern himself with its ability to think abstractly. To suggest that throwing encouraged that capability seems as nonsensical as to claim that Buddha and Newton were good jugglers, which led them to Buddhism and Newtonian physics. But natural selection is not constrained by our sense of what is nonsense.

Six hundred years ago Ibn Khaldun graphically defined abstract thinking as utilizing the pictures provided by the senses to make other pictures: "The ability to think is the occupation with pictures that are beyond sense perception, and the application of the mind of them for analysis and synthesis."[16] Throwing initiates a process *here-now* that produces an effect *there-then*. Throwers are causes disassociated spatially and even, for an instant, temporally from effects. We throwers are not forever and always immediately engaged with that which concerns us. We can be something apart, something other.

Hints of that can be found in hunting and fishing literature. In Norman MacLean's *A River Runs Through It*, a novella that pre-

---

[15] Calvin, "The Unitary Hypothesis: A Common Neural Circuitry for Novel Manipulations?" in *Tools, Language and Cognition in Human Evolution*, 232–42, 246–48; Calvin, "Did Throwing Sones Shape Hominid Brain Evolution?" *Ethology and Sociobiology*, Vol. 3 (1982), 115, 121.

[16] Ibn Khaldun, *The Muqaddimah*.

supposes "no clean line between religion and fly casting," the author writes of the perfect cast as

> so soft and slow that it can be followed like an ash settling from a fireplace chimney. One of life's quiet excitements is to stand somewhat apart from yourself and watch yourself softly becoming the author of something beautiful, even if it is only a floating ash.[17]

Homo sapiens are and, probably, hominids in general were superior to all other large animals in their ability to throw and also to cooperate, which evolutionary psychologist Paul M. Bingham judges to be "the ultimate source of human ecological dominance." He proposes that there may well be a connection between the two abilities.

The development of teamwork lagged in other creatures because they lacked the means to discipline their bullies and drones and prevent them from, so to speak, shouldering their way to the dinner table and displacing the team players. The latter could have fought to protect their interests, but that would have meant close combat with opponents of similar size and similarly sharp teeth and claws. The team players could have ganged up on the offenders, but such cooperation is undependable in combat where injury is likely. Standoff weaponry – stones, spears, arrows – especially if utilized by several throwers simultaneously, provided the solution to their problem. The team players won; the offenders joined the team or learned how to recruit their own teams. Either way our ancestors ascended the food chain and increased in numbers.[18]

---

[17] Norman MacLean, *A River Runs Through It and Other Stories* (New York: Pocket Books, 1976), 1, 47.

[18] For deeply informed consideration of this, see Paul M. Bingham, "Human Uniqueness: A General Theory," *Quarterly Review of Biology*, Vol. 74 (June 1999), 133–69.

Adapt to the will of the group in hunting, eventually in farming and the creation of religions and empires, or get pelted. According to examples in the Old Testament the standard punishment for individual nonconformism in the Bronze Age and early Iron Age was stoning, probably because that particular means was sanctified by thousands of generations of usage. Leviticus chapter 20, verse 27, informs us, for instance:

> Any man or woman among you who calls up ghosts or spirits shall be put to death. The people shall stone them: their blood shall be on their own hands.

The eighth book of the Gospel according St. John, in which Jesus famously recommends that he who is without sin should cast the first stone, finishes with his enemies taking up stones to kill his noncomformist self. He wisely disappears.[19]

Back to the Pliocene. Gorillas and the like were stuck with being what they were because they were herbivores and had to spend most of their waking time in eating huge quantities of leaves and such, huge because this food has low concentrations of nourishment per unit. Gorillas could never found civilizations. Our ancestors were omnivores, supplementing their vegetable diets with meat (decomposed or fresh), which provided a wider range of essential nourishments, fats and proteins, and in smaller packages than plant foods, enriching them with time to do more than just feed.

Meat comes in packages – haunches, livers – that are nourishing enough in relation to weight and size to justify being carried back to the rest of the family or band, unlike most vegetable matter. Meat comes in large solid pieces, unlike most vegetable matter, which requires containers. You can carry a leg of wildebeest on your shoulder for miles back to camp, but no more than a dozen

[19] St. John, 8: 7, 59.

beans until you invent some sort of receptacle. Meat spurred team-work. Lucky hunters could share their prizes with the unlucky, thereby making loyalty to the family and band practical – and then somebody with a full belly might have time enough to learn how to split and clean gourds and use them to carry beans.

* * *

Let us consider the effectiveness of rock throwing. We today are so impressed with complicated weapons like firearms and bows and arrows that we underrate that classic missile, the rock, and there-fore the ability of early hominids to effect change at a distance. A good baseball pitcher or cricket bowler can throw a ball (a sort of manufactured rock) at velocities as high or higher than 90 miles or 140 kilometers an hour. The impact of a missile at such velocities can crack ribs and even skulls. The impact of a dozen or so all at once would at the very least be discouraging.

Very recently; in terms of the time that hominids have lived on this planet, there were peoples so isolated from other humans that they had never acquired or had forgotten about bows and arrows and made little use of atlatls (more about which in a moment). Rocks fulfilled their need for missiles. The first European imperial-ists to come upon these groups thought them primitive in the extreme and, initially at least, as almost without effective weaponry. The invaders were often surprised.

In the fifteenth century the European invaders of the Canary Islands discovered at the cost of concussions and broken bones that the Guanches, natives of those islands, could "throw and wield a stone considerably more skilfully than a Christian: it seems like the bolt of a crossbow when they throw it." The Comte de La Pérouse in the eighteenth century sent a party of sixty-one ashore in the Navigators Islands (Tutuila, Samoa) for water, where they were received by Polynesians throwing rocks up to 1,400 grams in weight with "inconceivable vigour and address." The missiles were as effective as musket balls with "the advantage of succeeding one another with greater rapidity." Twelve of the landing party were killed.

Europeans found Hottentots, Fuegans, and Australian Aborigines to be as adept as rock deliverers as the Polynesians. "To fling one stone with perfect precision," wrote one European of Aborigines' skill, "is not so easy a matter as it seems, but the Australian will hurl one after the other with such rapidity that they seem to be poured from some machine."[20]

The earliest hominids may have made use of pebbles and boulders for tools, but we have no way of knowing until they began to chip and flake them to enhance their usefulness. The first of such tools, asymmetrical chunks of rock with sharpish edges, were the products of the hominid species or species that succeeded the Australopithecines. These stones were doubtlessly used for gashing through hide and flesh and possibly as missiles too, but we can't be sure.

Two million years ago, give or take the usual few hundred thousand, hominids with much larger brains than the Australopithecines appeared. They were not *Homo sapiens* – their big brains were not as big as ours – but they were in the conformation of their bodies and likely posture – long legs, short arms, unambiguously vertical stance, and so on – what we immediately recognize as human rather than apish.

These hominids developed, in time, a greatly expanded tool kit, including cleavers, picks, and the famous almond-shaped, bisymmetrical Acheulean "handaxes". Were some of them hafted to sticks to make the first axes and spears, that is, the momentous first two-part tools? Probably not, because they were flaked to a sharp edge all the way around, which would quickly wear through hafting. Were some of them projectiles? Why else would the mak-

---

[20] Barbara Isaac, "Throwing and Human Evolution," *The African Archaeological Review*, Vol. 5 (1987), 5–9.

ers go to the labor of providing a sharp edge all around so as to maximize chances of their striking the target with destructive effect? But they have an awkward shape for a projectile. So, of course, does a discus until you learn how to throw it.[21]

Whatever the purpose of these tools, the creatures who made them were unprecedented among large land mammals in their penchant for travel. They initiated what will be, until we migrate off our planet, the greatest of hominid diasporas, bursting out of Africa and deploying across Eurasia from England to Korea.[22]

They adjusted in whole or part to their new environments by hunting. Prey animals were present everywhere they might want to go and in all seasons, unlike the familiar food plants. To cite an analogous situation, how could *Homo sapiens* have moved into the Arctic and lived there year-round without meat?

These hominid migrants surely made use of missiles, but we have no decisive evidence that they or anyone else did until about 400,000 years ago, by which time somebody was making javelins.

In 1997 Hartmut Thieme reported on the results of a dozen years of digging in an open coal mine in Schöningen, Germany, at the northern end of the Hartz Mountains. He found rich troves of paleolithic flint tools, thousands of bones of water voles, beavers, deer, horses, bear, straight-tusked elephants, and others, some of the bones scored with the marks made with stone tools. These remains are carefully dated as upwards of 400,000 years old, that is, from a period when the region was still cooled by continental glaciers, and hominids, hard-pressed to obtain enough plant food during the short warm seasons to last the year-round, must have been dependent on hunting for survival.

---

[21] Roger Lewin, *Principles of Human Evolution: A Core Textbook* (Malden, MA: Blackwell Science, 1998), 343–8; Tattersall and Schwartz, *Extinct Humans*, 145, 167; William H. Calvin, *The Ascent of Mind: Ice Age Climates and the Evolution of Intelligence* (New York: Bantam Books, 1991), 177–86.

[22] *The Cambridge Encyclopedia of Human Evolution*, 352–3.

Among the artifacts are short, notched pieces of wood, possibly for the attachment of stone points. If so, these are parts of the oldest composite tools ever found. There are also burnt flints and reddened, cracked earth, possibly indications of what may be the oldest hearths ever discovered. Campfires may have been as essential in the cool climate as hunting. (More about fire in the next chapter.)

There were also at Schöningen three wooden poles from 1.8 to 2.25 meters long. They are the trunks of thirty-year-old spruce trees, the bark stripped off, the thick end sharpened. Their centers of gravity are about a third of the way back from the points. They are shaped and balanced like the spears thrown in the Olympic Games. To deny that they were made to be thrown, to call them digging sticks or snow-probes, says Professor Robin Dennell, would be like claiming that power drills are paperweights.[23]

Dennell celebrates the significance of these javelins in the history of hominid evolution with a new version of an old aphorism: "You are what you throw."[24] Their makers were the only sizable creatures on earth who did not have to commit their actual flesh to the immediate presence of harm in order to attack and defend.

There is much disagreement about precisely when *Homo sapiens* appeared – long after the Schöningen javelins, for sure. Archaic versions of us may have walked the earth a couple of hundred thousand years ago, if, of course, you accept such robust creatures as *Homo sapiens* and not just recent predecessors. One hundred thousand years ago humans as we know them were certainly around and about. They spread to Australia 50,000 years ago, and then to and through the length of America some thousands of years after that. They became, long before the industrial or even the neolithic revolution, the most widely distributed large animal on earth, and certainly the only one that could throw accurately.

[23] Hartmut Thieme, "Lower Palaeolithic Hunting Spears from Germany," *Nature*, Vol. 385 (February 27, 1997), 807–10; Robin Dennell, "The World's Oldest Spears," *Nature*, Vol. 385 (February 27, 1997) 767–8.
[24] Dennell, "World's Oldest Spears," *Nature*, Vol. 385 (February 27, 1997), 786.

They killed small and medium-sized animals and even preyed on big game; but let us be conservative in our speculation. To pitch a javelin into a mammoth with the unabetted strength of muscle alone requires getting dangerously close to the animal. Perhaps they dealt with the big ones decorously, stampeding them into swamps, off cliffs, and so on, and then pitched and thrust spears into them from positions of relative safety. Perhaps this is how, about 100,000 years ago, members of our species finished off a giant and now extinct buffalo, dug up not long ago at the mouth of South Africa's Klasies River with a spear point embedded in his neck.[25]

Our ancestors invented a new and better way to propel missiles in the Upper Paleolithic, a period of immense technological and general cultural acceleration that began about 40,000 years ago and ended 10,000 or 12,000 years ago with us careening toward civilization.[26] The same generations that left us the masterful cave painting of Lascaux and tons of meticulously flaked and specialized tools for dozens of purposes also left us the throwing stick (usually designated by its Aztec name, *atlatl*). With the atlatl, human hunters, only a few million years from the trees, killed some of the biggest mammalian meals that have ever lived on land during the incumbency of the genus *Homo*. One exuberant journalist has called the atlatl "the Stone Age Kalashnikov."[27]

For millennia hominids had made and used tools with stone, bone, and antler heads attached to wooden handles for convenience and to increase impact. The velocity of the business end of the tool was multiplied in proportion to the increase in its distance from the pivoting body parts: the pelvis, shoulder, elbow, and wrist.

[25] Dennell, "World's Oldest Spears," *Nature*, Vol. 385 (February 27, 1997), 767.

[26] John Pfeiffer, "The Emergence of Modern Humans," *Mosaic*, Vol. 21 (Spring 1990), 15–23. These dates, by the way, are European, not because everything started and ended there, but because more paleoanthropologists have lived and dug there than elsewhere.

[27] Kurt Kleiner, "Stone Age Klashnikov," *New Scientist*, Vol. 162 (May 15, 1999), 40–3.

The hominids who used these tools must have observed that when the head of an axe or hammer flies off in midswing, it does so with great velocity. They realized that if somehow a spear could be launched at the end of a handle, it too would travel a long way fast.

The odds are very high that the earliest example of a given kind of artifact discovered by an archeologist is not the first of that category ever made. The earliest wheel in our museums is much more likely to be the ten thousandth wheel than the first ever made. The earliest evidence of an atlatl we have, an antler hook, has been dated at about 17,500 years of age.[28] We are justified in speculating that the first atlatls were made long before that date. Shall we say 25,000 years ago? The device spread through the Old World and from there through the islands of southeast Asia to Australia, and through Alaska into North and then South America. Its diffusion is the best testimony of its effectiveness.

The problem of deciding on a date for the first atlatls is that they were and are usually made of wood, a material that, despite the Schöningen example, rots away swiftly. Furthermore, most of them were so simple in form that it is difficult to differentiate between them and other tools or simple debris. The atlatl at its crudest is a simple stick with a gutter in which to lay an arrow or dart, fletched (fitted with feathers) or unfletched, the butt edge of which rests against a hook or spur at the end of the stick. Most atlatls are about half again as long as the forearm of the individual who will use it. The atlatl approximately doubles the functional length of the thrower's rotating arm, multiplying the projectile's velocity. The projectile, usually called a dart, is usually twice as long as a standard arrow.

The atlatlist holds the atlatl at the other end from the spur rather as if it were a spear to be thrown, often with a finger curled over the top to hold the dart in place momentarily. The human whips the

---

[28] Pierre Cattelain, "Hunting During the Upper Paleolithic: Bow, Spearthrower, or Both?" in *Projectile Technology*, ed. Heidi Knecht (New York: Plenum Press, 1997), 214.

Use of the spear-thrower

Figure 2. A human hunter attacks a mammoth with atlatl and dart. Klein, *The Human Career* (Chicago: University of Chicago Press, 1989).

atlatl around in an overhand throw. The dart flies off as the atlatl extends out from the hand and arm.[29] We can see an approximation of this today as the jai alai player slinging his ball with his cesta (a long basket strapped to the arm) at velocities half again as fast as that of balls thrown by the best baseball and cricket players (Fig.2).

[29] William R. Perkins, "Archeological, Experimental, and Mathematical Evidence Supporting the Use of the Atlatl as a Primary Big Game Procurement Weapon of Prehistoric Americas," *Bulletin of Primitive Technology* (Fall 2000, No. 20), 71. Many experts are sure that the impetus of the dart is largely a matter of the flexing of said dart as it springs off the atlatl at an angle. For that controversy, see Perkins, 69–71.

The atlatl had greater significance than simply a new and effective means of getting food and providing offense and defense. It was the first evidence we have of a paleolithic conceptual revolution. The union of the throwing stick plus the dart may have have been the first human device with two moving parts. Others, with two and more and more parts, would follow.

Today an atlatl champion using carefully selected and machined equipment can consistently throw a dart more than 200 meters. In the nineteenth century, Australian Aborigine hunters using the *woomera* (their name for the atlatl) threw about half as far. Aborigines observed by Captain James Cook and his officers in the eighteenth century propelled darts "with a swiftness and steadyness truely surprising," hitting a target of unspecified size forty or fifty yard away, "with almost, if not as much certainty as we can do with a Musquet, and much more so than with a ball." Charles Darwin a half-century later watched as Aborigines "transfixed" a cap hung up at thirty yards with darts delivered by woomera. Australian indigenes tested for accuracy in the twentieth century consistently hit a wallaby-sized target at distances of twenty to thirty meters.[30]

The dart delivered by atlatl, perhaps twice as long as the usual arrow and a good deal greater in mass, was unquestionably effective against animals up to the size of goats and deer and humans. In the sixteenth century Spanish conquistadores declared that the most dreadful weapon of the soldiers of the Aztec and Inca empires were darts propelled by atlatls, which could pass right through an armored man. As for big game, which abounded in the Upper Paleolithic, stone projectile points have often been found in

[30] *The Journals of Captain James Cook on His Voyages of Discovery,* ed. J. C. Beaglehold (Cambridge: Cambridge University Press, 1955), Vol. 1, 396; *The Endeavour Journal of Joseph Banks, 1768–1771* (Sydney: Angus and Robertson, 1962), Vol. 2, 133; Charles Darwin, *Voyage of the Beagle* (Garden City: Anchor Books, 1962), 432; Cattelain, "Hunting During the Upper Paleolithic" in *Projectile Technology,* 218–19, 230; Kleiner, "Stone Age Klashnikov," *New Scientist,* Vol. 162 (May 15, 1999), 41.

Figure 3. A Native American about to launch a dart with an atlatl. "Address by Frank Hamilton Cushing," *American Anthropologist*, Vol. 8 (1895). By permission of the New York Public Library.

association with the bones of mammoths in North America, even between their ribs. These, of course, may have been thrust, not thrown, into the giant animals.[31]

In the mid-1980s Professor George C. Frison of the University of Wyoming experimented with using the atlatl to throw wooden darts with stone points into the carcasses of recently slaughtered elephants in Hwange National Park, Zimbabwe. The darts inflicted what would have been fatal wounds, often penetrating the interior cavities. Frison is satisfied that paleolithic humans could have hunted and killed mammoths. (Fig. 3) (Experiments

[31] Zelia Nuttall, *"The Atlatl or Spear Throwers of the Ancient Mexicans,"* *Archaeological and Ethnological Papers of the Peabody Museum* (1891), Vol. I, No. 3, 177; Alberto M. Salas, *Las Armas de la Conquista de América* (Argentina: Editorial Plus Ultra, 1986), 33–4; Bob Ortega, "Nifty Spear Flinger Aztecs Called 'Atlatl' Makes a Comeback," *Wall Street Journal*, (October 24, 1995), A1.

with living elephants in the wild should be pursued, he recommends, by persons younger and more physically fit than himself.)[32]

Upper Paleolithic hunters with atlatls and darts probably could have successfully attacked an land herbivore. (As for carnivores such as the saber-toothed tigers, what would have been the point of challenging those teeth and claws for that little meat?) Imagine a half-dozen hunters rising up out of the grass and flinging darts at high velocities into the body of a giant ground sloth, a target much bigger than a wallaby, perhaps forty meters away. Even if the physiological shock did not instantly overwhelm the animal, what was it to do? Where did the pain come from? When had pain ever come from a distance before?

Its reaction may have been like that of the two-dimensional protagonist of Edwin A. Abbott's *Flatland* who, when exposed to the third dimension for the first time, felt "an unspeakable horror."[33] I felt a lighter but similar dismay when I first learned that space and time stretched and shrank in Einstein's universe.

With the bow, humanity's next mechanical aid for throwing, the balance between hominids and the rest of the animal kingdom tilted even more sharply in favor of the former. The disadvantage of the atlatl in hunting and combat had been always been that the atlatlist, however stealthily he has stalked his prey, has to stand up, take one or two abrupt strides, and vigorously swing his arm overhead in order to deliver the dart. He has to provide the prey with at least a second or so of warning that something wondrous strange and possibly dangerous is under way. The dullest herbivore species will

---

[32] George C. Frison, "Experimental Use of Clovis Weaponry and Tools on African Elephants," *American Antiquity,* Vol. 54 (October 19, 1989), 766–7, 771–2; 773–7, 783.

[33] Edwin A. Abbott, *Flatland: A Romance of Many Dimensions* (New York: Dover Publications, 1992), 64.

eventually recognize the connection between the jack-in-the-box and the ensuing severe pain. The intended victim will bolt or, worse, attack. The archer, in contrast, can deliver from concealment an arrow at even higher velocity than the atlatl (though not necessarily with greater impact, the arrow being lighter than the dart).

The first bows must have been "self" bows, to use the technical name, that is, bows that are nearly straight until strung for use and made of only one kind of wood. The example of this simple bow that most of us are familiar with is the longbow of Robin Hood and his merry bandits. (There are other kinds, reinforced bows, composite bows, and so on,[34] which we will consider in a later chapter.) Wind-tunnel tests indicate that Robin Hood could, with a yew bow, fire an arrow 150 to 200 meters.

A good archer with the proper equipment can put an arrow through the hides of larger animals. A good archer can discharge an aimed arrow as often as every six seconds, and, if required to produce a torrent of arrows, can do so even faster than that. Henry Wadsworth Longfellow was taking only a limited exercise of poetic license when he proclaimed that Hiawatha could shoot ten arrows upward "with such strength and swiftness, That the tenth had left the bow-string Ere the first to earth had fallen!"[35]

A good archer is capable of great accuracy. On one occasion, according to chroniclers of Hernando de Soto's invasion of Florida in the sixteenth century, Amerindian archers, threatened by a swimming Spanish greyhound, in an instant put more than fifty arrows into its head and shoulders, the only parts exposed. Ishi, the California Yahi who stepped from the paleolithic into the industrial age early in the twentieth cen-

---

[34] Christopher A. Bergman and Edward McEwen, "Sinew-Reinforced and Composite Bows" in *Projectile Technology*, 146–7.

[35] Gareth Rees, "The Longbow's Deadly Secrets," *Scientific American*, Vol. 138 (June 5, 1993), 25; "The Arrow and the Song," *The Poems of Henry Wadsworth Longfellow*, ed. Louis Untermeyer (New York: Heritage Press, 1943), 24.

tury, could, after years of city life and little or no practice with the bow, consistently hit a target the size of a quail at twenty-five to thirty meters.[36]

It is difficult to date the first appearance of the bow and its arrows because they were, except for the stone and bone points, made of perishable material. Archaeologists have found quantities of small stone points in 20,000-year-old strata, declared them to be arrow points, and dated the bow in accordance with their appearance. Their logical deduction, however, may be wrong because hunters, before bows, may have simply discovered that small points on their spears increased penetration. At present, most experts date the earliest unambiguous evidence of bows and arrows at 10,000 to 12,000 years ago.[37] That was probably thousands of years after their invention and first use, which may have been as early as – oh, shall we revive the old guess of 20,000 years ago?

The invention spread rapidly through the eastern hemisphere, confirming its usefulness, but did not turn up in the Americas until as recently as perhaps a few thousand years ago. That may explain why the atlatl was still an important part of Aztec and Inca armament when the Spaniards arrived. When the English settled in Australia in 1787 the bow and arrow had not replaced the atlatl among the Aborigines, indeed, to all appearances hadn't arrived yet. The bow and arrow spread widely elsewhere in Oceania, but,

[36] Christopher A. Bergman and Edward McEwen, "Sinew-Reinforced and Composite Bows" in *Projectile Technology,* 144–47, 154; Gareth Rees, "The Longbow's Deadly Secrets," *New Scientist,* Vol. 138 (June 5, 1993), 24; Cattelain, "Hunting During the Upper Paleolithic" in *Projectile Technology,* 227; Garcilaso de la Vega, *The Florida of the Inca,* trans. John G. Varner and Jeannette J. Varner (Austin: University of Texas Press, 1951), 124; *Ishi The Last Yahi, A Documentary History,* eds. Robert F. Heizer and Theodora Kroeber (Berkeley: University of California Press, 1979), 193–5.

[37] Richard G. Klein, *The Human Career: Human Biological and Cultural Origins* (Chicago: University of Chicago Press, 1989), 375; Cattelain, "Hunting During the Upper Paleolithic" in *Projectile Technology,* 11.

oddly, the islanders' arrows were always unfleched and, therefore, inaccurate at any but short distances.[38]

※ ※ ※

We have been throwing this and that kind of missile for so many purposes and by so many means and for so many generations that the act has accreted all kinds of symbolic significance. It has even become part of the language. In our careers and our love affairs we are figuratively on target or off target. In defeat we throw down our arms; in defiance we throw down the gauntlet. Among peoples for whom the act of propelling missiles is a central life practice, it can be in itself a major means of expression, comparable to the way a pianist may reach out to strike a harmonious or a disharmonious chord to express approval or disapproval.

According to the Greek historian Herodotus, the Persians taught their boys only three things: to speak the truth, to ride, and to use the bow. When Darius the Great, emperor of the Persians, learned that the Athenians had burned Sardis, he took a bow, "set an arrow on the string, shot it up into the air and cried: 'Grant, O God, that I may punish the Athenians.'"[39] When two thousand years later Amerindians, shipped from Florida to Spain to be displayed, met a man who had participated in the invasion of their land, they resorted to their bows to cancel the language barrier:

> Then two of them (in order to make this man realize their desire to shoot arrows at him and the skill with which they might do so) discharged great arrows high into the air with so much force that they were lost from sight.[40]

---

[38] Cattelain, "Hunting During the Upper Paleolithic" in *Projectile Technology,* 220–1; Douglas L. Oliver, *Oceania: The Native Cultures of Australia and the Pacific Islands* (Honolulu: University of Hawaii Press, 1989), Vol. 1, 437.

[39] *Herodotus, The Histories,* trans. Aubrey de Sélincourt (London: Penguin Books, 1972), 57, 319.

[40] De la Vega, *The Florida of the Inca,* 641.

THREE

The Pleistocene and Holocene: "Cooking the Earth"[1]

Our intent entered the world as combustion.

Wendell Berry (1980)[2]

In the beginning, a long time ago, the creatures of the world did not have their present shape. One day Ngundid the snake, Mulili the catfish, Galaba the kangaroo and all other beings gathered in the country of the Rembarrnga people. From Maningrida way came Nagorgo, the Father, and his son Mulnanjini. They looked at all the creatures and said, "You are not proper people and not proper animals. We must change this." Then they made a ceremony which is still performed today. They lit a fire with their fire sticks which quickly spread until it engulfed all the beings and scorched the earth and rocks. When the fire subsided all

---

[1] The metaphor is Stephen J. Pyne's. See, for instance, *World Fire: The Culture of Fire on Earth* (New York: Henry Holt and Co., 1995), 14.

[2] *The Selected Poems of Wendell Berry* (Washington DC: Counterpoint, 1998), 122.

the creatures found that animals and humans had lost
their strange features and looked as they do now.

Australian Dreaming[3]

*H*ominids became colossi when they tapped the banked energies
of solar radiation, those recently stored in wood, leaves, and straw,
and those of the deep past, of peat, coal, and petroleum. Physicists
have accomplished something like this in our time by splitting and
fusing atoms and thus gaining access to atomic energy. Our paleolithic ancestors did so when they became chemists and learned to
manipulate for their own purposes the rapid combination of oxygen and other materials: fire.

When hominids joined other animals in the wake of wildfires
ignited by lightning and other natural phenomena to search for
roasted dainties, they didn't have to literally root through coals and
ashes. They used sticks to poke though coals and ashes. They took up
sticks burning at one end. They waved them to scare off rivals and
enemies. They brought them along to study fire's requirements, uses,
and dangers. Eventually, they learned to use their hands to produce
fire whenever they wanted by friction, by rubbing sticks together,
and by fire drill. An adept can do so in one to two minutes and has
been able to do so for many times over the age of the pyramids.[4]

Hominids thus became a force like rain or drought. "The ecological audacity of this act is staggering," proclaims Stephen J.
Pyne, our historian of fire and humanity: "it is as though a single
species laid claim to water or land or air."[5] Hence Zeus's displeas-
ure with Prometheus.

[3] *Australian Dreaming, 40,000 Years of Aboriginal History,* ed. Jennifer
Isaacs (Sydney: Lansdowne Press, 1980), 255–8.
[4] Hazel Rossotti, *Fire* (Oxford: Oxford University Press, 1993), 24.
[5] Stephen J. Pyne, *Vestal Fire: An Environmental History, Told through Fire,
of Europe and Europe's Encounter with the World* (Seattle: University of
Washington Press, 1997), 27.

It is very unlikely that the Australopithecines knew how to control fire. The javelin makers of Schöningen may have, but evidence for it is not convincing. If they did, they didn't make a common practice of doing so. Hearths, (i.e., places with soil baked by repeated fires and replete with hominid artifacts) don't show up in number until about 40,000 years ago as one of the identifying characteristics of the Upper Paleolithic revolution described in the last chapter.[6]

Manipulating fire was a specialty of the *Homo sapiens* species, and made the world a much easier place for humans to live in. Fire meant light in the dark; heat in the cold; the cooking of food; the discouraging of mosquitoes and flies; and the purposeful shaping and alteration of materials. Fire meant the capability to ward off carnivores, to drive prey, to transmogrify whole landscapes.

With fire humans could see in the dark, could live comfortably in the high mountains and poleward of the Tropics of Cancer and Capricorn. With fire humans could roast, parch, boil, steam, and fry, could pop maize, sear the legs off tasty grasshoppers, change rubbery squid into delicious calamari by seething it in its own ink or olive oil.

Most large animals are dependent on a limited number of kinds of food and starve when these run short. Cooking multiplied the kinds of nourishment available for humans. Only in the most difficult of times and outlandish environments have we been unable to find something we could eat. We can roast rhino neck meat and defang manioc of its toxins. Our talents as omnivores explain in large part our amazing success first in survival, then in migration, and ultimately in domination.

Many of our crafts and industries devoted to transforming raw substances into objects and materials of use had their start around the cooking fire. Pottery, ceramics, metallurgy – our very first industrial revolution – began with our ancestors squatting around

---

[6] *The Cambridge Encyclopedia of Human Evolution*, eds, Steve Jones, Robert Martin, and David Pilbeam (Cambridge: Cambridge University Press, 1992), 72.

and poking at fires. Aeschylus was close to the truth when he wrote, "All human arts are from Prometheus."[7]

∗   ∗   ∗

We take comfort from and love fire because it provides community. Campfires have to be tended, fed, disciplined – nurtured – which requires the tender loving care of cooperating hominids. In return, it provides its acolytes with all that we mean, including the connotations, by the word, *hearth*. The word "focus" means fireplace in the original Latin.

Wali Fejo of the Larrakia people of Australia remembered the excitement: "It was around the fires at night that many, many of the things of reality became meaningful. There was dance! There was song! There was story!"[8] John Keats caught the dreamy communion of gathering around fire in his poem "To My Brothers":

> Small, busy flames play through the fresh-laid coals,
> And their faint cracklings o'er our silence creep
> Like whispers of the household gods that keep
> A gentle empire o'er fraternal souls.[9]

Fire provided simple joy in and of itself. We love to set fires, all of us from Rocky Mountain Indians whom Lewis and Clark watched torching individual fir trees in 1806 to that daughter of Victorian England, Lady Mary Anne Barker, putting the match to grasslands in New Zealand a half century later:

---

[7] *Seven Famous Greek Plays*, ed. Whitney J. Oates and Eugene O'Neill, Jr. (New York: The Modern Library, 1938), 22.

[8] Wali Fejo, "Welcome Address" in *Country in Flames: Proceedings of the 1994 Symposium on Biodiversity and Fire in North Australia,* ed. Deborah Bird Rose, Biodiversity Series (Biodiversity Unit, Department of the Environment, Sport and Territories and the North Australian Research Unit, Australian National University, Australia), no pagination. http://www.ea.gov.au/biodiversity/publication/series/paper3/fire3.html

[9] John Keats, *Selected Poems*, ed. John Barnard (London: Penguin Books, 1988), 2.

It is a very exciting amusement, I assure you, and the effect is beautiful, especially as it grows dusk and the fires are racing up the hills all around us.[10]

Fire provided a halfway house wherein to meet and parley with the supernatural. All over Europe the great festivals – May Day, Easter, Midsummer, and the others – were celebrated with bonfires. Typically, the celebrants began by extinguishing all the fires in some broad locality and then in the dark created new fires, often by the most ancient means, friction, on the hilltops for all to see. Then fires could be renewed everywhere.

The sight of the fires wrung from novelist Thomas Hardy a passage of Victorian grandiloquence: "These tinctured the silent bosom of the clouds above them and lit up their ephemeral caves, which seemed thenceforth to become scalding caldrons." Bedazzled peasants danced round the fire through the night and leaped through the flames to be cleansed, to gain health and good fortune, to marry soon, to give birth to many children.[11]

According to the Aztecs' calender, every fifty-two years all of creation rolls to the brink of extinction. At that crisis they extinguished all fires in their empire and waited in the dark for a renewal of that creation as manifested in fire. A priest spun a fire drill in kindling gathered in the opened chest of a well-born captive and created fresh flames. Runners carried brands and embers from that tiny source throughout the empire, renewing fires everywhere.

At that time the common folk came to the flame, hurled themselves at it, and blistered themselves as fire was taken.

---

[10] *The Journals of Lewis and Clark,* ed. Bernard DeVoto (Boston: Houghton Mifflin Co., 1953), 409; Lady Barker, *Station Life in New Zealand* (Auckland: Penguin Books, 1987), 195.

[11] James George Frazer, *The Golden Bough: A Study in Magic and Religion* (New York: Book League of America, 1929), Vol. 2, 609–49; Thomas Hardy, *The Return of the Native* (New York: Bantam Books, 1981), 13–14.

When the fire had been swiftly distributed everywhere among them, there was a laying of many fires; there was a quieting of many hearts.[12]

Perhaps the similarities of the European and Aztec fire ceremonies arose from the nature of fire, which can be killed and revived and spread everywhere like the influence of gods. Or perhaps these two peoples were simply practicing variants of primordial tradition. If so, that tradition must have been ancient indeed because these two could have shared no common history since well before the end of the last Ice Age and the flooding of the Bering Strait.

It was that association of fire with magic and restoration of health and life force that would lead humans, perhaps inevitably, to gunpowder, as we shall see in Chapter Six.

With fire humans could practice "terraforming," which *The Oxford English Dictionary,* looking into the future, defines as the act of transforming a planet into something like the earth, "especially as regards suitability for human life."[13] We have done the job with one planet already, our own, and a good deal of that before we had planted our first field.

The archaeologist and naturalist Rhys Jones calls our paleolithic terraforming "firestick farming,"[14] that is, the purposeful use of

[12] Fray Bernardino de Sahagún, *Florentine Codex: General History of the Things of New Spain, Book 7, The Sun, Moon and Stars, and the Binding of the Years,* trans. Arthur J. O. Anderson and Charles E. Dibble (Santa Fe, NM: The School of American Research and the University of Utah, 1953), 25–9; Michael D. Coe, *Mexico,* 3d. ed. (New York: Thames and Hudson, 1984), 161.

[13] *The New Shorter Oxford English Dictionary by Historical Principles,* ed. Lesley Brown (Oxford: Clarendon Press, 1993), II, 3256.

[14] Rhys Jones, "Firestick Farming," *Australian Natural History,* Vol. 16 (September 1969), 224–8.

broadcast fire to shape environment.[15] His homeland, Australia, is a good place to undertake an investigation of firestick farming, still practiced by millions today, and as we practiced it in all continents but Antarctica throughout all but the last few moments of human history. There the evidence is relatively fresh because there the paleolithic lasted until the arrival of crop seeds, horses, the alphabet, and gunpowder with British settlers in 1788. And there the evidence is starkly clear because so much of that continent is dry and flammable.

The sight of a long unburned landscape is as disturbing to the Australian Aborigine firestick farmer as that of an unweeded garden is to a gardener. Firestick farming is not a matter of casual ignitions, like an urbanite's incineration of trash, but of a fire master selecting the moment, location, and fuel in order to stall one or more natural process and stimulate others by means of small fires, big fires, cool fires, hot fires. His fiery bushmanship is exercised not now and then and crudely, but often and with discrimination in much the same way a good gardener hoes, manures, and waters (and, we can conjecture, as an expression of a universal human pleasure in setting fires).[16] He makes mistakes – Australia bears fire scars – but millennia of practice have trained him to minimize the number and magnitude of those mistakes. Australia is the better for his work "as regards suitability for human life."

Yinirrakun, also known as April Bright, of the Mak Mak Marranunggu people of Kurrindju puts it this way: "If you don't look after country, country won't look after you."[17] The Aborigines

[15] *The New Shorter Oxford English Dictionary by Historical Principles,* ed. Lesley Brown (Oxford: Clarendon Press, 1993), II, 3256.

[16] Henry T. Lewis, "Ecological and Technological Knowledge of Fire: Aborigines versus Park Rangers in Northern Australia," *American Anthropology,* Vol. 91 (December 1989), 947–9. For another informative discussion of this subject, see Timothy F. Flannery, *The Future Eaters: An Ecological History of the Australasian Lands and People* (New York: George Braziller, 1995), 217–36.

[17] April Bright, Mak Mak Marranunggu, "Burn Grass" in *Country in Flame,* no pagination.

use fire to minimize ground cover for snakes and other varmints. They use it to open up the bush so they can move about more easily.[18] They burn to eliminate the wet season's massive biomass before it becomes fuel for explosive and very dangerous wild fires.[19] Louise Meredith wrote in Tasmania in the 1840s that landscape she knew there had once been "a great park." Then came the expulsion of the native Tasmanians and the end of firestick farming: "And now, look at it! Terrible bloody stuff! Thick bush everywhere and these terrible fires coming through every now and then."[20]

The Aborigines burn to open the landscape to encourage the propagation of food animals – kangaroo, wallaby, emu, cassowary – and, when the time comes to harvest, then to drive them into ambush.[21] They burn to create landscapes in which food plants will spontaneously prosper. The botanist Peter Latz of Alice Springs in the arid center of the continent, who grew up with and learned firestick tactics from the Arrernte Aborigines, estimates that they got about one-third of their food from firestick management of the land. He personally fancies a kind of desert raisin, a Solanum relative of the potato and tomato, which pops up after the burning off of spinifex. "Bloody good tucker!" says he.[22]

The Aborigines sear the land and thus, paradoxically, encourage biodiversity. Lightning ignites fires, but only occasionally. Without the firestick, much of the landscape is smothered in the heavy growth of a relatively few species. There is less savanna

---

[18] Rhys Jones, "Mindjongork: Legacy of the Firestick" and R. W. Braithwaite, "A Healthy Savanna: Endangered Mammals and Aboriginal Burning" in *Country in Flames*, no pagination.

[19] David Bowman, "Why Skillful Use of Fire Is Critical for the Management of Biodiversity in Northern Australia" in *Country in Flames*, no pagination.

[20] Jones, "Mindjongork: Legacy of the Firestick" in *Country in Flames*, no pagination.

[21] Stephen J. Pyne, *Burning Bush: A Fire History of Australia* (New York: Henry Holt and Co., 1991), 96.

[22] Peter Latz, "Fire in the Desert" in *Country in Flames*, no pagination.

with its abundance of species. The firestick opened up the soil to direct sun and to the sprouting of endemic fire-tolerant species.[23]

The poet Mark O'Connell recommends that patriotic Australians use the firestick as an act of botanical patriotism:

> Bright petals follow, as if you'd scattered
> fifty packets of English seed; but not one
> has a name Shakespeare knew...[24]

Australian Aborigines in particular and humans in general, with a few exceptions like the Eskimos, for tens of thousands of years have been pyro-enthusiastists. Our ancestors used fire to terraform, creating "cultural landscapes" radically different from what would have existed without the firestick.

The most obvious are those where fire-tolerant flora, especially grasses, followed the flaming firestick into forests and occupied the land. The Mediterranean littoral, the womb environment of Western civilization, the lands of the Jews, Greeks, Romans, Phoenicians, Catalans, Carthaginians, their friends and enemies, provides examples of the advance of the grasses, led by fire and enforced by axe and close-cropping livestock. Their fire-makers exploited the annual dry seasons to initiate the massive change of what was mostly woodland into a humanized landscape of low trees and scrub, bare ridges, eroded hillsides, ravines, and narrow valleys.

Few examples of pre-firestick landscape survive along the anciently seared littoral except for a few patches on the slopes of Lebanon and Mount Athos. These, sacred groves and therefore off-limits to wielders of the firestick, are soughing remainders of a Mediterranean coast that was once forested.[25]

---

[23] Braithwaite, "A Healthy Savanna" in *Country in Flames*, no pagination.

[24] Mark O'Connell, "Firestick Farming" in *Country in Flames*, no pagination.

[25] Pyne, *Vestal Fire*, 85. See also John Robert McNeill, *The Mountains of the Mediterranean World: An Environmental History* (Cambridge: Cambridge University Press, 1992).

So was the east coast of New Zealand's South Island when humans, the Maori, first arrived. Their crops, all tropical, did poorly on the South Island, and so these Polynesian pioneers, in order to facilitate hunting the giant Moa and other fauna, burned off the antipodal forest. When the British came ashore in the nineteenth century, the east coast littoral was grass and ferns.[26]

Ten and twenty thousand and more years ago members of the *Homo sapiens* species, furnished with firestick, atlatl, and latterly, many of them, with bow and arrow, were the most dangerous, adaptable, and widespread of all large land animals. They were equipped to be the champion imperialists of their entire phylum, to solve problems abruptly and, if necessary or if simply so inclined, by broadcast violence.

As the continental glaciers withdrew, humans' history became their own and not just a subdivision of the planet's. And so, for us, it becomes appropriate to shift from measurements of time in terms of geological change to those referring to human behaviors.

It is 40,000 years ago and we enter the Upper Paleolithic, the late Stone Age. Hominids, inferior to their rivals and enemies in strength and speed, are superior to all others in ballistic and incinerational capabilities. The authors of Genesis, when their time comes, will credit this to the will of God:

> Then God said, Let us make man in our image and likeness to rule the fish of the sea, the birds of heaven, the cattle, all wild animals on earth, and all reptiles that crawl upon the earth.[27]

---

[26] Pyne, *Vestal Fire*, 428; Alfred W. Crosby, *Ecological Imperialism: The Biological Expansion of Europe, 900–1900* (Cambridge: Cambridge University Press, 1986), 222.

[27] Genesis 1.

FOUR

The Upper Paleolithic: "Humans and Other Catastrophes"[1]

We live in a zoologically impoverished world, from which all the hugest, and fiercest, and strongest forms have recently disappeared; and it is, no doubt, a much better world for us now they have gone. Yet it is surely a marvellous fact, and one that has hardly been sufficiently dwelt upon, this sudden dying out of so many large mammalia, not in one place only but over half the land surface of the globe.

Alfred Russel Wallace (1876)[2]

When did we become unmistakably *us*, a species of creatures who, properly dressed, would not attract attention in the streets of Tokyo or New York? A second question: when did we become creatures, who, given suitable instruction, could take a job in an

[1] This is the title of a symposium on Pleistocene extinctions held at the American Museum of Natural History in New York in April 1997.
[2] Donald K. Grayson, "Nineteenth-Century Explanations of Pleistocene Extinctions: A Review and Analysis" in *Quaternary Extinctions: A Prehistoric Revolution,* eds. Paul S. Martin and Richard G. Klein (Tucson: University of Arizona Press, 1984), 29.

office in either city? There is disagreement among the experts as to the answer to the first question, about when *Homo sapiens* – hominids with femurs and clavicles and spines and skulls shaped like ours – first appeared, but all agree that it was no less than 100,000 B.P. (years Before Present).[3]

The answer to the second question has been harder to produce. Evidence of anatomy survives in bones, but evidence of behavior often doesn't survive at all. Did *Homo sapiens* 100,000 B.P. or more *act* like us? Apparently not, if the size and complexity of tool kits and the rate at which they grew and changed are the measure. Their kits were, relative to what was to happen next, small and changed slowly for half of the millennia of *Homo sapiens*'s existence. We were a new kind of hominid, but in comportment not too terribly different from our predecessors.

Then, in the late Pleistocene, starting about 40,000 B.P. (give or take the paleoanthropologist's "standard deviation" of some thousands this way or that), the acceleration that brought us to our current situation began. The factor that sparked this acceleration may have been the completion of the evolution of language from simple signals to the miraculous vehicle of expression (i.e., vocabulary *plus syntax*) that it is today. The most recently contacted peoples in the highlands of New Guinea have languages as adaptable and capable of subtleties as that of the symbolist poets or corporation attorneys, which suggests that speech as we currently know it is considerably older than civilization. Fifty thousand years old seems a good guess.

About then the number of the kinds of our tools increased, their crafting refined, and stagnancy of design gave way to a rolling variation from region to region and time to time. Clothing improved – some of it fitted and sewn – and so did housing, some of it utilizing mammoth bones. We began trading amber, seashells,

---

[3] These are not solar years, but radiocarbon years. The two are similar enough for my purposes, if not for scientific purposes.

and special kinds of flint over long distances. Sculpture and painting, much of it astonishingly artful, appeared. Religion advanced,
as evidenced by multiple burial sites with carefully made grave
goods. We invented the atlatl and then the bow and arrow, and utilized fire frequently and skillfully. We migrated faster and farther
than ever before, into Australia, northern Eurasia, and, eventually,
across into the Americas.[4]

We achieved something unprecedented in the history of life on
the planet. We became very good at substituting cultural evolution
for genetic. We had become us.

This period of progress, population increase, and geographical
expansion for the *Homo sapiens* species in the late Pleistocene was
– coincidentally? – one of general disaster for many others. Scores
of species and even dozens of genera disappeared. Nothing quite
this devastating had happened in millions of years, nothing more
spectacularly devastating in tens of millions of years.[5]

There are many aspects of this extinction event that are distinctive. One, as just mentioned, was its magnitude. Two, it hit big
animals much harder than small. Upwards of half of all the world's
genera of mammalian "megafauna" – animals with adult weights
over forty-four kilograms (one hundred pounds) – disappeared.
When the die-off ended, all land mammals of one metric ton or
over, of which there had been numbers of species – mammoths,

[4] Richard G. Klein, *The Human Career: Human Biological and Cultural
Origins* (Chicago: University of Chicago Press, 1989), 360–84.
[5] Ian Tattersall, "Once We Were Not Alone," *Scientific American,* Vol. 282
(January 2000), 56–62; Ian Tattersall and and Jeffrey Schwartz, *Extinct
Humans* (New York: Nevraumont Publishing Co., 2000), 224; Paul S. Martin
and David W. Steadman, "Prehistoric Extinctions on Islands and Continents"
in *Extinctions in Near Time: Causes, Contexts, and Consequences,* ed. Ross
D. E. MacPhee (New York: Kluwer Academic/Plenum Publishers, 1999), 17;
John Alroy, "Putting North America's End-Pleistocene Megafaunal
Extinction in Context" in *Extinctions in Near Time,* 121; Anthony John
Stuart, "Late Pleistocene Megafaunal Extinctions: A European Perspective"
in *Near Extinctions,* 257.

mastodons, ground sloths, woolly rhinoceroses, giant kangaroos, and more – were gone, except in southern Asia and sub-Saharan Africa. More kinds of megafauna were lost than have been lost since, despite our population explosion, leveling of forests, industrialization, and so on.

Three, whatever it was that drove whole genera over the brink of extinction, it did not kill off ocean animals. Whales, for example, seem not to have been affected, though they and other aquatic animals had clearly suffered losses in the earlier periods of extinctions.

Four, the megafauna that disappeared in the late Pleistocene did so without being directly replaced, an oddity. Extinctions usually have happened when one species outpropagates or outcompetes another for nourishment, that is, when one displaces another from its niche in the ecosystem. The displacer and displacee are often similar in important ways, as would have been the case if, for instance, Old World horse species had displaced New World horse species. But that isn't what happened. American horses disappeared utterly and were not replaced until Europeans brought in horses from across the Atlantic about 10,000 years later. The existence of an open niche for horses is confirmed because European horses went feral soon after arrival and increased into the millions.

Five, this extinction event did not affect all continents equally. The New World lost seventy-four entire genera (*not* species) of megafauna. "It is impossible," wrote Charles Darwin, "to reflect on the changed state of the American continent without the deepest astonishment. Formerly it must have swarmed with great monsters: now we find mere pigmies, compared with the antecedent, allied races."[6]

---

[6] Martin and Steadman, "Prehistoric Extinctions on Islands and Continents," in *Extinctions in Near Time*, 17–19; Editors, "The Mammoth's Demise," *Discovering Archaeology*, Vol. 1 (September–October 1999), 34; Charles Darwin, *The Voyage of the Beagle* (Garden City: Anchor Books, 1962), 174.

Australia lost more than the Americas in proportion: fifteen out of its sixteen genera of vertebrate megafauna, including giant reptiles as well as marsupials. Europe and northern Asia came through the late Pleistocene better, but not unscathed, losing, for instance, 37 percent of its megafaunal herbivores. We don't have good statistics yet for southern Asia, but we can say that its losses, though considerable, were less than those previously mentioned: elephants and tigers, alive and kicking, certainly qualify as megafauna. Africa came through better than any other continent, as a trip to its game parks today will prove.[7]

Six, the late Pleistocene extinctions happened on the continents, not on islands with their small and therefore vulnerable ecosystems. For instance, flightless Hawaiian birds survived until the termination of their isolation thousands of years later.

Seven, the late Pleistocene extinctions were not simultaneous. Those in the Americas happened about 11,000 years ago, possibly in as few as 400 years. The megafaunal extinctions in Australia are harder to date, but appear to have been concentrated about 50,000 years ago. The extinctions of the giants in Africa and Eurasia were scattered across tens of thousands of years. The mystery thickens if more recent megafaunal extinctions, those of Madagascar and New Zealand, of the former's elephant bird and the latter's moa, are included. These giants disappeared abruptly

---

[7] Martin and Steadman, "Prehistoric Extinctions on Islands and Continents" in *Extinctions in Near Time,* 17–19; Norman Owen-Smith, "The Interaction of Humans, Megaherbivores, and Habitats in the Late Pleistocene Extinction Event" in *Extinctions in Near Time,* 58–9; Donald A. McFarlane, "A Comparison of Methods for the Probabalistic Determination of Vertebrate Extinction Chronologies" in *Extinctions in Near Time,* 102; Gifford H. Miller et al., "Pleistocene Extinction of *Genyornis newtoni*: Human Impact on Australian Megafauna," *Science,* Vol. 283 (January 8, 1999), 205.

a couple thousand years or so ago or less – yesterday, in comparison to the other departures.[8]

Scientists have attempted to explain the mystery of the late Pleistocene extinctions ever since it came to their attention toward the end of the eighteenth century. Georges Curvier proposed rapid changes, catastrophes of one kind or another. Charles Lyell proposed slow changes, the kind that raise and lower mountain ranges. As the nineteenth century rolled on, a few and then a few more began to take seriously the thought that human hunters might have been the cause. Among them was Darwin's great colleague, the co-founder of the modern theory of evolution, Alfred Russel Wallace. He was sure, he wrote, "that the rapidity of ... the extinction of so many large Mammalia is actually due to man's agency" – and then he hedged, as have many since – "*acting in co-operation with those general causes* [his italics] which at the culmination of each geological era has led to the extinction of the larger, the most specialised, or the most strangely modified forms."[9]

For Wallace, as for us, the chief problem in thinking about this mystery is that our minds cannot quite wrap all the way around the idea of these megafaunal extinctions. Nothing like them, in their sum, has ever happened in recorded history. The Steller sea cow, that ten-ton arctic relative of the manatee, was killed off in

---

[8] Martin and Steadman, "Prehistoric Extinctions on Islands and Continents" in *Extinctions in Near Time*, 18; McFarlane, "A Comparison of Methods" in *Extinctions in Near Time*, 102; R. N. Holdaway and C. Jacomb, "Rapid Extinction of the Moas *(Aves Dinorithiformes)*: Model Test and Implications," *Science*, Vol. 287 (March 24, 2000), 2250–4; Thomas Higham, Atholl Anderson, and Chris Jacomb, "Dating the First New Zealanders: The Chronology of Wairau Bar," *Antiquity*, Vol. 73 (June 1999), 420–7; For New Zealand, also see the chapter with the incomparable title, "There Ain't No More Moa in Old Aotearoa," in Timothy F. Flannery, *The Future Eaters: An Ecological History of the Australasian Lands and People* (New York: George Braziller, 1995), 195–8.

[9] Grayson, "Nineteenth-Century Explanations of Pleistocine Extinctions," *Quaternary Extinctions*, 9–15, 20–9.

the eighteenth century, but there were only a few of them and they made up only one species of megafauna, not scores.

The lesson of our *recorded* experience is that it is hard to extinguish a numerous and widely spread animal species. Extinction has been the fate of many creatures in the last few hundred years, but usually of animals restricted to islands, like the dodos of Mauritius. The fate of these thousands of stupid, flightless birds would seem to have little to tell us about the extinction of what must have been millions of gigantic mammoths across continents. They fell victim to hungry sailors with clubs.

After Wallace's generation – he died in 1913 – paleontologists and scientists in related fields tended to turn their attention to mysteries that offered the hope of more finely grained, testable solutions than did this paleolithic Götterdämmerung. Then, in the 1960s, Professor Paul S. Martin of the University of Arizona produced the first of a series of books and articles that have obliged colleagues and laypersons alike to reconsider the extinctions.[10] The debate has been fulminating ever since.

Stiff-necked biblicists still issue ex cathedra pronouncements crediting the megafaunal tragedy to The Flood. Other more loosely jointed authorities offer such limber concepts as "genetic senility." Fortunately, there are in addition tightly reasoned theories based on physical evidence. Most of these can be arranged under two headings, the climatic and the anthropogenic.

The Pleistocene epoch, the last one before our own Holocene, lasted from about one and a half million to 10,000 years ago. Characteristic of this stretch of time was a series of advances and

---

[10] His bibliography is long. I suggest starting with his "40,000 Years of Extinctions on the 'Planet of Doom'" in *Palaeogeography, Palaeoclimatology, Palaeoecology* (Global and Planetary Change Section), Vol. 82 (1990), 187–201; and *Quaternary Extinctions: A Prehistoric Revolution* (Tucson: University of Arizona Press, 1984), which he and Richard G. Klein edited.

retreats of continental ice sheets, with accompanying descents and ascents of sea level and opening and closing of land connections between continents and islands. There may have been a correlation between these glacial maneuvers and periods of faunal extinctions.

At the peak of the last Ice Age a great deal of North America and northwestern Eurasia was under kilometers of ice; sea level was low, Alaska and Siberia were joined, as were New Guinea and Australia; and rivers of ice descended from temperate zone and tropical mountain ranges. About 20,000 years ago the climate began to warm and the continental ice sheets to retreat. The change was not steady but episodic, with shifts – warm, cold, dry, wet.

Those who tout climate change as the cause of the late Pleistocene extinctions argue that this warming trend diminished the area in which the plants on which the megafaunal herbivores had evolved to feed upon could survive. Indeed, it is true that the "mammoth steppes," the semi-arid vastnesses in the middle of North America, did shrink. The biggest herbivores with the biggest appetites – and the carnivores who fed on them – died out the fastest. As the megaherbivores, who were terraformers like elephants today, rooting out water holes and knocking over trees, disappeared, whole ecosystems changed and sources of food and shelter for smaller animals disappeared, and then so did these creatures.

The opponents of climate theory offer several counterarguments. There had been a number of ice ages and inter-ice ages in the Pleistocene, but only in its final millennia were there so many extinctions. Why? If global warming had caused them, why the loss of so many more species and more abruptly in the Americas and Australia than in Eurasia and Africa? There must have been some other factor than climate.

Furthermore, climate change cannot have caused the extinctions because it, though comparatively abrupt, was far from instantaneous. There was nothing like a winter spreading swiftly across the planet with a shroud of smoke and debris after collision with a comet. The North American and Russian mammoth steppes, for example, did not disappear in a day or a decade – nor, for that matter, did they entirely disappear at all. Their flora, the fodder plants of the cold-climate giant herbivores, retreated with the cold climate into the mountains and north toward the arctic. Woolly rhinos should have diminished in numbers and disappeared from the middle latitudes, but survived in the northern. As for Australia's megafaunal extinctions circa 50,000 B.P., there is little evidence for pronounced climatic changes in that continent then, and none contemporaneous with the extinctions in Madgascar and New Zealand.[11] We must look for some factor other than climate.

This almighty other factor, the only one of significance some insist, was humanity, which was able to adapt to new situations more quickly via culture than their prey could via genetics, and was therefore able to hunt the megafauna to death. This, the anthropogenic or overkill theory, supposes that hunters preferred the biggest herbivores, rather than minor animals, because they were the biggest packages of meat available. Then the big carnivores died off for lack of prey, along with smaller animals dependent on the megafauna in one way or another.

The megafaunal species of the Old World survived the human onslaught better than their equivalents elsewhere because, the theory goes, they and the hominids had evolved together in Africa and Eurasia. When advanced hunters appeared in the Old World with improved weapons and tactics, the effects on the megafauna were

[11] H. Gifford Miller et al., "Pleistocene Extinction of *Genyornis newtoni*": Human Impact on Australian Megafauna," *Science,* Vol. 283 (January 8, 1999), 207. For a different interpretation, see E. Esmee Webb, "Megafaunal Extinctions: the Carrying Capacity Argument," *Antiquity,* Vol. 27 (March 1998), 46–55. For another consideration of this subject, see Timothy F. Flannery, *The Future Eaters: An Ecological History of the Australasian Lands and People* (New York: George Braziller, 1995), 180–94, 199–207.

drastic. Europe and northern Asia lost eleven out of forty-three species of megafauna.[12] But as a group these giants, compared to the naïfs overseas, had less of a mental leap to adapt to the new situation. The Old World hulks had to learn that these familiar bipeds were now dangerous, but they didn't have to realize that they actually existed – or that it was not advisable to lumber over to have a look at them. The survivors were among those who had less to learn.

Humans per se may or may not have arrived in the Americas before the extinctions – that is a matter of controversy – but it is clear that the extinctions there took place as big game hunters, the knappers of the famous Clovis points, arrived and spread widely some 11,000 B.P.[13] The latest research supports estimates of 50,000 B.P. for Australia's megafaunal extinctions, that is, just about when humans walked in across the flats or paddled in from New Guinea.[14] The megafaunal disappearances in New Zealand and Madagascar, much more recent and therefore easier to date, coincide nicely with the debarking and spread of human beings. (Lest you might think that last settles the question, I should point out that island ecosystems are relatively small and the impact of exotics, human or otherwise, is always enormous. The megafaunal extinctions in New Zealand and Madagascar may prove nothing more than that.)

The anthropogenic theory has it that whenever or wherever these immigrant human predators arrived, they were enormously

[12] Anthony John Stuart, "Late Pleistocene Megafaunal Extinctions" in *Extinctions in Near Time*, 261.

[13] Anna Curtenius Roosevelt has supplied a nice summary of all this in "Who's on First? There Still No End to the Controversy Over When and How Humans Populated the New World," *Natural History*, Vol. 109 (July–August 2000), 76–8.

[14] H. Gifford Miller et al., "Pleistocene Extinction of *Genyornis newtoni*": Human Impact on Australian Megafauna," *Science*, Vol. 283 (January 8, 1999), 205–8.

successful, propagated abundantly, and continued slaughtering prodigally, eliminating many species and even whole genera.

The theory that humans were responsible for the megafaunal extinctions of the late Pleistocene provides respectable answers to the various submysteries of the major mystery and holds together logically, but many are not satisfied with it as an explanation for the mystery as a whole. It just seems silly to maintain that people, of whom there were few as compared to their alleged prey, killed off millions and millions of giant and dangerous animals, so many as to eliminate them utterly from the planet. The humans simply did not have the technology to kill such quantities of megafauna. "Fancy attacking a rhinoceros," Searles Wood challenged over a century ago, "whose hide will turn a rifle bullet, with a flint hatchet or a bone skewer!"[15]

Perhaps the first thing to do in judging the anthropogenic theory is not to ask if humans actually caused the extinctions, but *could* they have, that is, is or is not the proposition silly? First of all, were there enough humans, especially on their frontiers, to accomplish the slaughter? Common sense (which is often myopic and bumptious) says no, but arithmetic says yes. Paul S. Martin and James E. Moisimann propose a detailed scenario, which I offer in brutal simplification for brevity's sake.

Their scenario begins with one hundred humans emerging from a glacial corridor leading down from Alaska to Edmonton, Alberta, into a region with a megafaunal density at least that of a present-day African game park. The arrivistes kill one 450-kilogram animal per week per human, more than needed but not more than you would expect of nouveaux riches who would be eating only the choicest bits. Their population increases by as much as 3.5 percent annually, a high but not unknown rate in our day and one that we might expect of our very successful hunters. Adults

[15] Grayson, "Nineteenth-Century Explanations" in *Quaternary Extinctions*, 30.

live longer, women conceive and bring to successful birth more children, and the newborn live to become adults and reproduce themselves. The frontier, fueled by megafaunal meat, sweeps forward and fans out laterally. The speed of advance depends on the estimates of game density, human life expectancy, and so on that you feed into your reconstruction of the hunters' debut in North America. In a thousand years *at most,* according to all versions, the frontier stretches in a long arc from Atlantic to Pacific and deep into Mexico. There are many thousands of proto-Amerindians in North America, and no megafauna left beween Edmonton and the human avant-garde.[16]

This is a computer model: its North America is like a bathtub in which the contents rise and fall in exact accordance with the diameter of the drain. Nothing, certainly not a continent and its ecosystems, is that simple. But the model does demonstrate that human hunters *could* have accomplished the late Pleistocene extinctions in North America and, plausibly, at other frontiers, assuming they had the means.

What about the hunters' means, their weaponry, which Wood demeaned as no more than flint hatchets and bone skewers? The matchup of humans versus megafauna was not as uneven as he thought. First, there are always fewer bigger than smaller animals. Wiping out mammoths would have been easier than wiping out mice. Also, the megafactor of megafauna, size, is not as important as it appears at a glance. A hunter is no deader for being stamped to death by a 1,000-kilogram than a 100-kilogram behemouth. Indeed, it may be easier to dodge the former than the latter.

Tactics can be more important than size. Pleistocene hunters were surely the equal of the nineteenth-century South African indigenes who, armed with no better than spears, hunted elephants successfully. Sometimes they would select one elephant, break it

---

[16] James E. Mosimann and Paul S. Martin, "Simulating Overkill by Paleoindians," *American Scientist,* Vol. 63 (May–June 1975), 304–13.

loose from the herd, hurl spears into it, goad it to run in order to increase blood loss and fatigue, trail it, hurl more spears, trail it on and on for as long as it might take to dispatch it.[17] A dangerous business for the hunters, true, but they had more practical knowledge about the pertinent aspects of elephant physiology and psychology than any zoologist does today.

We know that the ancient hunters often harvested megafauna the safe way, by driving them over cliffs, for instance, and we can be sure that if confrontations were necessary, the hunters seldom challenged adults in fighting prime. Like all sensible carnivores, they would have attacked the young, the sick, the old, the pregnant. They were surely as epicurian in their choices as the gauchos and Amerindians of the pampa in the eighteenth century, who, when the season was right, would kill two pregnant wild cows apiece a day for the pleasure of eating their fetuses, a true delicacy.[18]

The hunters did not take on the megafauna *mano a mano*. They may have used poisonous projectiles against big game, as the twentieth-century !kung of Africa have successfully.[19] But we should not try to make too much of this. Hunters moving through new lands may not have known what plants, insects, and so on to utilize for poisons.

They certainly attacked from a distance by throwing javelins and flinging darts at high velocities with that essential item in the late Pleistocene hunter's kit, the atlatl. If today a hobbyist with an atlatl can throw darts through automobile doors, then lifetime hunters could throw darts though megafaunal hides 11,000 years ago. As Professor Frison's experiments have demonstrated, darts

[17] Gary Haynes, *Mammoths, Mastodons, and Elephants* (Cambridge: Cambridge University Press, 1991), 298.
[18] Letter from Barbara G. Beddall, *Science*, Vol. 180 (1 June 1973), 905.
[19] Andrew W. Johnson and Timothy Earle, *The Evolution of Human Societies: From Foraging Group to Agrarian State* (Stanford: Stanford University Press, 1987), 47.

propelled with atlatls can break elephant bones and penetrate internal cavities. Ipso facto, a single human daredevil with an atlatl and a handfull of darts might have attacked a mammoth or mastodon or ground sloth and just possibly have won. A team of cooperating hunters usually would win.

Homo sapiens everywhere at the end of the Pleistocene had fire as a weapon, a servant, an entertainment. There is no reason to doubt that they wielded the firestick any less deftly than Australian Aborigines in the twentieth century. Fire would have driven megafauna as effectively as any other animals. There is a nineteenth-century description of 500 east Africans, utilizing a surely ancient tactic, encircling eighteen elephants with fire and then harvesting them with showers of spears.[20]

Repeated fires ten millennia back would, as today, have altered the landscape faster, at least locally, than many megafauna could adapt. The evidence that Maori used fire against the New Zealand forest, thereby destroying moa habitat, is plentiful.[21] The evidence elsewhere is not so unequivocal: the archeologist cannot differentiate between an accumulation of charcoal left by a natural fire and one left by an anthropogentic fire.

The megafauna were not so well equipped to deal with the *Homo sapiens* threat as we might think. We are so visually dependent that we forget that, for many animals, Africa's white rhinoceros, for instance, the nose is more important than the eye. If you want to photograph a white rhinocerus, come to him from downwind and he won't run until he hears the shutter's click. A Pleistocene hunter stalking weak-sighted megafauna would have had little problem with getting close enough to them to launch darts.

The experience of some animals over the ages has been such as to encourage behaviors that work against the usual and time-honored

[20] Haynes, *Mammoths, Mastodons, and Elephants* 297.
[21] Richard N. Holdaway, "Introduced Predators and Avifaunal Extinction in New Zealand" in *Extinctions in Near Time*, 218.

carnivores, but have disastrous effect when the enemy is human. For example, musk oxen don't flee attackers. They "circle the wagons," the bulls forming a circle facing out around the young and the most vulnerable oxen. The hungry wolf feints this way and that, finds no breach in the wall of horns, snarls, and lopes away. The human hunter stands back and launches his missiles at will. The circle gets smaller and smaller and smaller.[22]

Many species do not recognize threats as such until the experience of many generations teaches them to. Dodos and Great Auks are extinct because hungry sailors could walk right up to these innocents and brain them. In the nineteenth century, hunters with no equipment deadlier or more far-reaching than harpoons (javelins) were able to row up to prodigiously dangerous megafauna, whales, and kill so many thousands as to bring whole species to the brink of extinction.[23] Many whales still haven't learned to be afraid of humans, as anyone who has been on a successful whale-watch excursion knows.

Today in African game parks the big and dangerous animals ignore humans if they stay in their motor vehicles, which are new to the wild species. Only if the bipedal tourists get out, and by that act manifest themselves as a familiar threat, will the animals run or attack. Why would megafauna on the human frontiers of the late Pleistocene have looked upon such bipeds as anything worth fearing? Being big can be a disadvantage if it makes one blasé.

Big animals have long gestation periods – elephants twenty or so months, humans nine – and therefore low birth rates. They can-

---

[22] Norman Owen-Smith, "The Interaction of Humans, Megaherbivores, and Habitat in the Late Pleistocene Event" in *Humans and Other Catastrophes* (New York: American Museum of Natural History, 1998), http://amnh.org/science/biodiversity/extinction/Day 1 PresentationFS.html, no pagination.

[23] D. H. Cushing, *The Provident Sea* (Cambridge: Cambridge University Press, 1988), 141–52; Louwrens Hacquebord, "Three Centuries of Whaling and Walrus Hunting in Svalbard and Its Impact on the Arctic Ecosystem," *Environment and History*, Vol. 7 (May 2001), 177–8.

not ward off threats to their existence by producing myriads of off-spring, a random few of whom are bound to survive. They must adapt by changing behaviors. Proliferation often works better than intelligence: thus our kitchens swarm with roaches and our grasslands and savannahs are empty of mammoths.

There is in this era of AIDS and fears of Ebola pandemics an au courant epidemiological supplement to the anthropogenic theory. Humans did not arrive in the New World and Australia unaccompanied. They and whatever creatures that may have accompanied them – other migrant animals, semidomesticated dogs, body lice, whatever – came with microlife on board, tiny invaders that the incumbent life forms would have been poorly prepared to resist. Perhaps the arrival of humans and their entourage set off panzootics.

Such events have happened in the modern period. Rinderpest appeared in sub-Saharan Africa for the first time in the 1890s, probably brought into Somalia by the Italian army and swept south, wiping out most of East Africa's domestic stock and hordes of wild ungulates. In 1950 the Australians imported the disease myxomatosis in the hope that it would kill off their multitudes of imported rabbits. It didn't quite, but did eliminate millions. The several diseases that Europeans carried across oceans to their colonies, smallpox most famously, sped on ahead of the imperialists and eliminated large portions of the indigenes of the Americas, Australia, and Oceania before many of these unfortunates had ever seen a white man.[24]

A new infection could have killed a lot of individual animals in a brief period, but it is unlikely that one kind of infection would

[24] Pule Phoofolo, "Epidemics and Revolutions: The Rinderpest Epidemic in Late Nineteenth-Century Southern Africa," *Past and Present*, No. 138 (February 1993), 112–43; William H. McNeill, *Plagues and Peoples* (Garden City: Anchor Press/Doubleday, 1976), 56–7; Alfred W. Crosby, *Ecological Imperialism: The Biological Expansion of Europe, 900–1900* (Cambridge: Cambridge University Press, 1986), 195–216.

have affected members of so many different species. There are broad spectrum diseases, rinderpest, for instance, that infect cattle, goats, sheep, and similar wild animals – but not all or even most mammals. Myxomatosis is a rabbit disease exclusively, and it does not even affect all kinds of rabbits. AIDS is a human disease and while its virus can infect other primates, they don't die. Perhaps there were several devastating panzootics at a time in the late Pleistocene? But what infection or, if you want, infections would have preferentially affected big animals and left smaller animals relatively untouched?

There is no physical evidence supporting the exotic germ theory at present, but microscopic and molecular investigations undertaken with this in mind may turn up something presently.[25]

None of the theories about the cause of the late Pleistocene extinction event seems adequate for all the examples cited. Proponents of climate causation provide no satisfactory answers to questions as to why this change would have been so much deadlier than earlier ones, or why it would have killed megafauna almost exclusively, or why the dates of the extinctions should have been different in different parts of the world.

The anthropogenic theorists are asking us to believe that relatively few humans with no better than the firestick, spears, darts, and, latterly and less than universally, bows and arrows, were responsible directly for the deaths of millions of animals under wildly varying circumstances. The theory works well for Australia,

[25] Ross D.E. MacPhee and P.A. Marx, "The 40,000-Year Plague: Humans, Hyperdisease and First-Contact Extinctions" in *Natural Change and Human Impact in Madagascar* (Washington, D.C.: Smithsonian Press, 1997), 169–217; Holdaway and Jacomb, "Rapid Extinction of the Moas *(Aves Dinorithiformes)*: Model Test and Implications," 2250–4; Higham, Anderson, and Jacomb, "Dating the First New Zealanders: The Chronology of Wairau Bar," 420–7.

New Zealand, and Madagascar – all islands, if big ones, where the ecosystems were especially vulnerable to exotic invasions – but what of the vast continents of the Americas? The New World was so bereft of megafauna when Europeans arrived that the Comte de Buffon and other early naturalists thought there must be something intrinsically inferior about the New World.[26]

Scientists in general prefer to test for one factor at a time. That way unambiguous measurements can be taken and precise comparisons made. Otherwise, the number of possibilities goes exponential and the effort is more like politics than bench science. If scientists frame a model of the Pleistocene extinctions that incorporates *all* these causes, excepting only the Noachin flood and genetic senility, then they and we will have a opaque and lumpy stew. What we all want is a clarified broth.

But reality *is* a stew. Perhaps the reason that no single one of the standard theories for the extinctions seems fully satisfactory is that no one factor could have done the job everywhere the megafaunal exinctions took place. Perhaps the change in climate *and* the arrival of human hunters with atlatl and firestick at roughly the same time explains what happened in the New World. Perhaps something like that happened in Australia, too, but we need more evidence and better dating there before we can make up our minds. The purely anthopogenic theory seems most likely for New Zealand and Madagascar.[27] There possibly may have been the factor of new diseases in any and all of these cases.

There was in them all a new or unprecedentedly perseverant predator, the human hunters. They were perseverant, as pointed

---

[26] Henry Steele Commager and Elmo Giordanetti, eds., *Was America a Mistake: An Eighteenth-Century Controversy* (Columbia: University of South Carolina Press, 1968), passim.

[27] Holdaway and Jacomb, "Rapid Extinction of the Moas *(Aves Dinorithiformes)*: Model Test and Implicaions," 2250–14; Higham, Anderson, and Jacomb, "Dating the First New Zealanders: The Chronology of Wairau Bar," 420–7.

out in Chapter Three, in that they were omnivorous, especially so after they learned to cook. If they killed off most of a given prey species, they did not starve and fall in numbers themselves, but just switched to other food sources and lived to kill off the few survivors of their original prey whenever they happened to come upon them. The human hunters were new in that they could strike from afar and manipulate fire. Their weapons were unprecedented and so, presumably, was their harvest.

In the nineteenth century, whalers hunted the Pacific grey whales, though the animals earned the nickname of devilfish for their penchant for fighting back. The hunters ambushed them in the lagoons of Baja California, where genetics and millennia of experience dictated that these megafauna should come to breed and bring forth their calfs, and in a few decades brought the species close to extinction.[28] When the whales' number dropped so low that it was more expensive to find them than the whalers could earn from killing them, the hunting stopped. If it had continued to be profitable, whalers would have wiped them out. Can we believe that Pleistocene hunters would have been any more softhearted?

Subtle differences in the bones of Neanderthal and early *Homo sapiens* hands, currently interpreted as indicating that the latter were better at using hafted weapons than the former, also suggest that humans were better at manipulating atlatls. That may help to explain why humans are the sole survivors of the hominid clan, which, as is common for successful lineages, grew from small beginnings into an ensemble of species, and, then, as is uncommon and chilling, shrank down to a solitary one in the Upper Paleolithic.[29]

---

[28] Charles M. Scammon, *The Marine Mammals of the North-western Coast of North America* (New York: Dover Publications, 1968), 22–8.

[29] Wesley A. Niewoehner, "Behavioral Inferences from the Skhul/Qafzeh Early Modern Human Hand Remains," *Proceedings of the National Academy of Science, USA,* 10.1073/pnas.041588898. A neat discussion of this can be found in Joao Zilhao, "Fate of the Neanderthals," *Archaeology,* Vol. 53 (July–August 2000), 24–31.

Human hunters' capabilities were a matter of cultural, not genetic, evolution and were therefore relatively abrupt in their application, perhaps with dreadful consequences for their own species. Animals, who kill in direct contact with their victims, rarely slaughter large numbers of their own species. They have inborn controls that stay the coup de grâce in fights with kin. Humans, who kill with tools, especially missiles, do not. Matt Cartmill has put it succinctly: "When a defeated wolf goes belly up, the victor turns away with instinctive chivalry: when a defeated man goes belly up, the victor spears him in the belly."[30]

Homo sapiens is arguably the only species that commits genocide, which, we might note, might easily extend in practice to species suicide.

[30] Matt Cartmill, "Four Legs Good, Two Legs Bad," *Natural History*, Vol. 92 (November 1983), 75.

FIVE

From Weapon Craftsmanship to Weapon Technology

> Your right hand shall show you a scene of terror: your
> sharp arrows flying, nations beneath your feet, the
> courage of the king's foes melting away.
>
> Psalms 45:4–5 (First Millennium B.C.E.)

> The fashion of the Greek fire was such that it came
> frontwise as large as a barrel ... and the tail of fire that
> issued from it was as large as a large lance. The noise it
> made in coming was like heaven's thunder. It had the
> seeming of a dragon flying through the air.
>
> Geoffrey de Villehardoüin (1150?–1218?)[1]

As the continental glaciers retreated and the interglacial phase
we enjoy began, members of the *Homo sapiens* species were in
occupation of all the inhabitable continents. They performed
rough surgery on their ecosystems, and then, a few millennia after

---

[1] Geoffrey de Villahardouin and De Joinville, *Memoirs of the Crusades*,
trans. Frank T. Marzials (New York: E. P. Dutton, 1958), 186.

the death of the last woolly rhino, began, as farmers and pastoralists, to create, willy-nilly, their own ecosystems.

Among the earliest to do so were the peoples of southwestern
Asia and adjacent northern Africa. They lived in a region in which
radically contrasting environments existed in a few or a single day's
walk of each other – mountains and flatlands, river valleys and
deserts – offering provocation and opportunity for biological
experimentation. They lived at the juncture of the African and
Eurasian continents, and at the near juncture of the Mediterranean
and the Indian Ocean. They lived at the crossroads in the world,
where cross-fertilization of the fresh and exotic was maximal.

They invented the earliest civilizations[2] and quickened similar
developments to east and west, where like latitudes and roughly
similar climates were propitious for the spread of their crops and
the growth of similar political forms, the city-state and then the
empire. The small grains of southwest Asia, for example, became
staples of both the Roman and Han populations and emperors
ruled both. Innovative societies sprouted from the China Sea to the
Atlantic. There were such societies elsewhere – Mesoamerica and
the Andes, for instance – but this Old World lineup would be, in
itself and in its exchanges with peoples on its frontiers, the source
of humanity's most widely adopted agricultural systems, religions,
political forms, and technologies for thousands of years.[3] This was
in its sum *the* Hearthland of world civilization, and I shall here-
after refer to it as that.

The peoples of the Hearthland, like all peoples, were addicted
to projectile technology. Of the ballistic devices – post-atlatl and

---

[2] Civilization is a saltpeter of a word, often triggering explosive arguments. I
use it not in moral comment, but simply in reference to peoples settled in
cities, villages, hamlets, and to the kinds of political, economic, social, and
military structures associated with such populations.

[3] William H. McNeill, *The Rise of the West: A History of the Human
Community* (New York: New American Library, 1963), 322–6.

post – bow and arrow – they invented or were among the earliest to adopt the one that has received the most publicity: the sling, the preferred weapon of David of the Old Testament. It is no more than a pocket, leather in most cases, with strings attached to opposite sides of the pocket. The object to be slung is placed in the pocket, the slinger takes up the sling by the ends of the strings, whirls it over his or her head a few times, and then releases one of the strings. The missile, usually about thirty grams in weight, flies off at speeds in excess of one hundred kilometers an hour.[4]

The advantages of the sling are its cheapness and simplicity, the ready availability of its missiles, and their velocity. David's missiles were five smooth stones picked up from a brook.

> He put his hand into his bag, took out a stone, slung it, and struck the Philistine on the forehead. The stone sank into his forehead, and he fell flat on his face on the ground.[5]

So much for Goliath, a *mano a mano* bruiser, who had encountered an expert in projectile technology.

The sling had long been in use in the Neolithic and, I would guess, in the late Paleolithic, as well, but the evidence is hard to come by. A sling, the bag and strings, rots away even faster than atlatls and bows. The lead slugs made for use with the sling (because they are heavier in proportion to their wind resistance than stones) can be easily identified, but they appeared late in the history of the weapon. Whatever the date of the sling's inception, it was employed extensively by David's time, late Bronze or early Iron Age, and slingers were still important in armies a millennium and a half later, as Xenophon, circa 400 B.C.E., makes clear in *Anabasis*. The Spaniards whom Hernán Cortés led into Mexico had to fend off missiles launched by sling as

[4] Nikos Vutiropulos, "The Sling in the Aegean Bronze Age," *Antiquity*, Vol. 65 (June 1991), 280, 284.
[5] I Samuel, 17.

well as atlatls. When Captain Cook voyaged through the Pacific in the eighteenth century, he found that Polynesians used the sling.

But it was inevitable that archers would displace slingers. The motion of someone using a sling requires as much space and time as that of someone using an atlatl. A slinger cannot hunker down and shoot. A slinger cannot conveniently use his weapon while on horseback. A slinger can achieve accuracy only if he practices from childhood on, as David the shepherd did in protecting his flock from predators. The archer should start young too, but a mediocre archer will hit the proverbial barn door more often than a mediocre slinger. He can sight along his arrow before firing, while the slinger depends on what we can almost call intuition to select *exactly* the right infinitesimal fraction of a split second to release the string.[6] It is a feat that only a creature with brachiating ancestors could even hope to manage. David's feat in hitting a target as small as a forehead, while he and the owner of the forehead were both moving, deserves all the publicity it has received.

But despite David's celebrity, the future lay with the bow and arrow as an individual projectile weapon because of its already cited advantages and because it was a device that admitted improvement. Proofs of the significance of that future linger in the plentiful presence of such names as Archer and Fletcher in our telephone books a full eight centuries after firearms began to displace the bow.

The power of the bow is the energy that is stored in the bow (and, perhaps, some in the string) when the archer nocks an arrow to the string and draws it back. The stiffer bow, the greater that energy, but the strength of the human muscles engaged in drawing a bow is strictly limited. Bowyers finessed that problem by finagling the bow.

The power of a given bow, assuming its springiness as a constant, is proportional to the area circumscribed by two lines. One

---

[6] Vutiropulos, "The Sling in the Aegean Bronze Age," 284.

line represents the bow in its relaxed and unstrung position and the other line the string when it is pulled back to firing position. The bigger the area between the lines, the greater the velocity of the arrow.

The simplest way to increase that velocity is to maximize the circumscribed area. The earliest and simplest bows – they are called self bows – consisted of a string and one long stave of a homogeneous material, usually some kind of wood. This bow's power is a matter of its length (again, assuming its elasticity as a constant). The longer the bow the greater the area between the lines described and the greater the velocity of the arrow.

Today the self bow most of us know best is that of medieval England, the kind that western Europeans used almost to the exclusion of other kinds until the spread of the crossbow.[7] The draw weights of examples of this bow made for adult males, the amount of pull that these archers had to produce, ranged from an impressive forty-five to an amazing eighty kilograms. (Could the latter have been fired by men on their backs with their feet pressed against the bows?) That muscle energy was collected and retained for instantaneous utilization in a *long* bow, as the English called it, a bow about as long as the archer was tall. Such a bow is inexpensive and could deliver up to ten aimed arrows a minute.

But the self-bow was a weapon with limited prospects. It propelled an arrow quite hard enough to kill food, but what about an enemy of your own species with a shield or leather or metal armor, and how much longer could a long bow be before its draw length exceeded the archer's arm length? How deftly, to get down to combat realities, can you use such a weapon from horseback or for firing through a slit in a castle wall?[8]

---

[7] Bert S. Hall, *Weapons and Warfare in Renaissance Europe: Gunpowder, Technology, and Tactics* (Baltimore: Johns Hopkins Press, 1997), 18.

[8] Gareth Rees, "The Longbow's Deadly Secrets," *New Scientist*, Vol. 138 (5 June 1993), 25; John K. Thornton, *Warfare in Atlantic Africa, 1500–1800* (London: UCL Press, 1999), 10.

The material of a bow is subject to distorting forces. Flexing the bow to fire an arrow stretches its back (the side away from the archer) and compresses its belly. The back starts to pull apart and splinter (the splinters are called slithers) and the belly to crinkle (the crinkles are called frets or crystals).[9] Either or both phenomena will ruin a bow, a problem that bow makers in many parts of the world tried to solve in prehistory by fashioning bows of more than one material, composite bows. They cut themselves a self-bow and then fixed sinew to its back with animal or fish glues, increasing its elasticity by several times over, and stiffened the belly with horn or some other dense hard substance resistant to compression. Such a bow can be considerably shorter than a long bow, with little if any reduction of arrow velocity, and thus be as deadly while much more manageable.

Another variation is the reflexed bow. It is not straight or evenly curved when unstrung and relaxed, but like a letter "S" that continues on and makes one more curve before stopping. Extreme versions of the reflexed bow in unstrung posture may nearly touch their tips with their backs compressed and bellies stretched, opposite to their configurations when strung (Fig. 4). The area between lines representing the unstrung bow and the bow's string when ready for use, and, therefore, the power to be stored in such a bow when drawn, is considerably greater than in an evenly curved bow of similar length. The Arabian archers who marched with Xerxes and the Persians in their invasion of Greece carried bows of this kind. Herodotus mentions that these relaxed into reverse curves while unstrung.[10]

The masterpiece of the traditional bowyer's art is the reflexed composite bow. Its core is typically wood, the back sinew, the belly

[9] Vernard Foley, George Palmer, and Werner Soedel, "The Crossbow," *Scientific American*, Vol. 252 (January 1985), 104.
[10] *Herodotus, The Histories*, trans. Aubrey de Sélincourt (London: Penguin Books, 1996), 397.

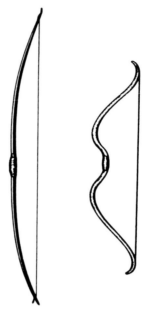

Figure 4. A self or long bow and a reflexed composite bow.

horn. When unstrung it has a configuration very different, close to the opposite, of its strung conformation. It is shorter than a self bow of equivalent power or even than a bow, again of equivalent power, that is only reflexed or reinforced. This bow is difficult to make and a challenge to string – it can jerk itself out of the archer's hands and unilaterally reassume the relaxed position – but it is compact and powerful and worth the problems it poses.[11]

Odysseus possessed a massive example of one of these bows, which he left behind when he sailed for Troy. Not one of Penelope's suitors could manage it, but when her husband finally returned he quickly strung it, drew it with ease, and plucked the

[11] Edward McEwen, Robert L. Miller, and Christopher A. Bergman, "Early Bow Design and Construction," *Scientific American*, Vol. 264 (June 1991), 80.

string, which "Twang'd short and sharp like the shrill swallow's cry."[12] Penelope's suitors quailed – advisedly.

The composite reflex bow was especially valuable for horsemen, who needed a bow both mighty and wieldy. Indeed this bow may have been first made for mounted warriors, possibly the Assyrians, as long ago as the third, certainly the second, millennia B.C.E., somewhere in or near the Asian grasslands.[13] The Parthian shot, made from horseback, was surely delivered with a reinforced reflex bow. Genghis Khan conquered most of Eurasia with cavalry armed with these bows.

The composite reflexed bow is as fine a projectile weapon as craftsmen can produce using organic materials – wood, sinew, horn. The Ottoman Turkish bowyers, usually credited as being the greatest of all time, provided Sultan Selim III with such a bow that in 1789 he used to shoot an arrow 889 meters. The arrow was probably one of the light "flight" variety, but even so the distance is astonishing – even unbelievable.[14]

Wood, sinew, horn, and the human muscle can do no better than (or as well as) that without mechanical chicanery. Bowyers resorted to the latter to produce the crossbow, probably first in China about the fourth century B.C.E. and certainly no later than the second century B.C.E. A crossbow consists of a stiff bow fixed across the end of a length of wood or metal called a tiller. The

---

[12] *The Odyssey of Homer in English Translation by Alexander Pope* (Norwalk, CT: Easton Press, 1978), Bk. XXI, 317; Joseph Needham and Robin D. S. Yates, *Science and Civilisation in China*, V, *Chemistry and Chemical Technology*, Pt. VI, *Military Technology: Missiles and Sieges* (Cambridge: Cambridge University Press, 1994), 102–3.

[13] Christopher A. Bergman and Edward McEwen, "Sinew-Reinforced and Composite Bows: Technology, Function, and Social Implications" in *Projectile Technology* (New York: Plenum Press, 1997), 144–7, 152–4.

[14] Bergman and McEwen, "Sinew-Reinforced and Composite Bows" in *Projectile Technology*, 144. See also Ralph Payne-Gallwey, *The Crossbow: Medieval and Modern Military and Sporting* (London: The Holland Press, 1995), 27–30.

string is not drawn directly by hand, but by means of a device that enlists the strength of the legs and back, a stirrup, for instance, or, for the stiffest bows, a winch or some similar mechanical aid. The arrow, often of metal and properly called a bolt (if square headed, a "quarrel"!), is nocked to the bowstring and set in a trough or some such support on the tiller. It is shorter than the usual arrow and not uniformly slim but tapered so it is wider at the unpointed end. It may not be fletched at all but dependent on wind resistance, stronger at the broad tail than the sharp point, to keep its path straight. The string is released to send the bolt on its way by some sort of trigger (Fig. 5).

A fourteenth-century French crossbow owned by the museum of the U.S. Military Academy at West Point has a bow a meter and a bit wide, a tiller not quite as long, and bolts about thirty-eight centimeters in length. It is not much more awkward to carry and manipulate than a standard infantry rifle of our recent wars. It was especially handy for defense: a crossbow is far more convenient to use from behind walls and parapets than an atlatl and even a regular bow.

Another of its major advantages is the ease with which a greenhorn can be instructed in its use. Hitting a barn door at fifty paces is a skill easy to acquire with a normal bow, but it requires practice from childhood on if the archer is to consistently hit smaller targets. He or she must pull the string and arrow back and take aim and release, all without wavering or jerking, though arm, back, and chest and even leg muscles are maximally contracted or extended.[15]

The challenge is obliquely indicated by an ancient Chinese formula for success in bowmanship: "The left hand should be as if

---

[15] Thomas Esper, "The Replacement of the Longbow by Firearms in the English Army," *Technology and Culture*, Vol. 6 (1965), 382–93.

Figure 5. Reflexed composite bows and crossbows employed in execution of a saint. Antonio Pollaiudo, *The Martyrdom of St. Sebastian*. Alinari/Art Resource, New York.

pushing away a stone, and the right hand as if leaning on a branch; when the right hand releases [the arrow] the left hand should not know – this is the Tao of archery."[16]

The skeleton of an archer recovered from Henry VIII's *Mary Rose,* which sank in 1545, provides clear evidence of the effort required. The bones of his left forearm, upper backbone, and right hand, just those you would suspect would be affected by drawing heavy bows, are deformed.[17]

The crossbowman has to exert himself to draw the string, but then can relax as he sights down the tiller and squeezes the trigger. If he aims at a distant target, the tiller, which he will have to tilt up, will obscure his view, but all in all his challenge is not much greater than a rifleman's. The new bow proved so valuable in war that those skillful in its use earned highest esteem and in Spain even knighthoods. England's Richard I, *Coeur de Lion,* an especially strong proponent of the weapon, was killed by a bolt from one at a siege in Aquitaine in 1199.[18]

The crossbow's big disadvantage compared to the usual bow is that its rate of fire is much slower, but its power and the weight and velocity of its missile compensated for that, especially after its makers shifted from composite to steel bows. A draw pull of forty-five kilograms for a long bow seems close to the limit for practical use in hunting or combat. One large crossbow has tested at 550 kilograms; it cast a bolt 420 meters. With such weapons the defenders of the Chinese frontier outmatched frontier raiders with even the best composite reflex bows. The Chinese even made crossbows that fired several bolts at once and repeating crossbows with bolts stacked in magazines so as to drop into firing position as, one by one, they were dispatched.

[16] Needham and Yates, *Science and Civilisation in China,* 111. Vol. 5, pt. 6.
[17] Hall, *Weapons and Warfare,* 20.
[18] Payne-Gallwey, *Crossbow,* 46, 48,

The power of the crossbow allowed common soldiers to consistently put bolts through knightly armor, which may account for the Second Lateran Council's anathematization in 1139 of the device against any but infidels. Confucianists, also proponents of class stability, may have had their doubts about it too, but also to no avail. The crossbow was the preeminent projectile weapon for the individual soldier across Eurasia for centuries. Hernán Cortés took a company of crossbowmen with him to Mexico and not because he was an antiquarian.[19]

The steel crossbow was an excellent weapon, and, more important than that for us, it was a harbinger of a trend in military technology that changed the nature of warfare and has continued to our day. It was a thing of levers and cogs and steel. It was a machine.

Around and after 1,000 B.C.E., technology began to displace craft in missile propulsion. The enemies most worth concerning oneself about often hid behind walls. What was needed was a missile system for beating down walls (or, alternatively, to keep wall-beaters at a distance from one's own walls). A new and hugely important profession arose, that of the military technician.

Peoples from the Mediterranean to the China Sea had long since developed artillery that tapped the same source of energy as their handheld bows, that is, the elasticity of certain materials. There were several kinds of these: arcuballistas, ballistas, catapults, mangonels, and onagers, with definitions that shifted with different locations and times.[20] (We aren't, by the way, any neater in our nomenclature: e.g., our tanks can't go anywhere unless we fill up their tanks.)

[19] Foley, Palmer, and Soedel, "The Crossbow," 104–10; Needham and Yates, *Science and Civilisation in China*, 121, 125, 140, 143, 147, 148, 156, 160, 170, 174, 178–83.
[20] Payne-Gallwey, *The Crossbow*, 249–50.

All of these big projectile launchers rested on their own bases, though the smaller of them were often little more than giant composite bows or crossbows. The later and bigger ones had stocks (levers for heaving the missiles) inserted in tightly twisted bundles of sinew or hair. The stocks were hauled back, commonly by winch, against the resistance of the bundles of fibers to increasing torsion. They were then released, the stock snapped forward, and the projectile – perhaps an arrow several meters long, perhaps a boulder – soared away. Such were the engines that King Uzziah of the Old Testament ordered to be placed on the towers and bastions of Jerusalem "to discharge arrows and large stones."[21]

The torsion engine was a contrivance of distinctly finite utility. Its maximum range and throw weight were unextendably set by the strength and elasticity of the materials of the fibers of the bundles, which varied with the weather and wore out fast. This engine shares these shortcomings with a child's rubber-band slingshot. The successor, the trebuchet, emerged in the middle of the first millennium C.E.[22]

The trebuchet can be described as a large-scale combination of the atlatl and David's favorite projectile launcher. It is simply a long beam pivoted on a fulcrum much closer to one end than the other, with the object to be thrown in a sling fixed to the long end. The earliest of these engines, probably Chinese, are called traction trebuchets. They were powered by one man or, usually, several men pulling down on ropes fixed to the end of the beam closest to the fulcrum. At the other end someone held the sling with the missile. At the instant of maximum pull, usually as his feet were leav-

---

[21] 2 Chronicles 26:15; Werner Soedel and Vernard Foley, "Ancient Catapults," *Scientific American*, Vol. 240 (March 1979), 150–60; E. W. Marsden, *Greek and Roman Artillery: Historical Development* (London: Oxford University Press, 1969), 1, 16–33, 35; Payne-Gallwey, *The Crossbow*, 259–60.

[22] Needham and Yates, *Science and Civilisation in China*, 184–7; W. T. S. Tarner, "The Traction Trebuchet: A Reconstruction of an Early Medieval Siege Engine," *Technology and Culture*, Vol 36 (January 1995), 141–4.

ing the ground, he let go; the long end went round, and off went the missile.

At least as early as the first half of the twelfth century C.E. someone, a Muslim probably, replaced the gang of pullers with a heavy weight, a major improvement because dependence on human muscle set a strict limit on how big the machine could be. Ten or twenty ropes and pullers, even thirty, might work, but a hundred ropes would be a mare's nest and that many pullers would be falling all over each other. Weight was universally available (a box of dirt would do) and could be depended on to fulfill its function every time – that is, to be heavy. If something heavier yet was wanted, add more dirt, rocks, or what-have-you.

Pull down the long end of the beam of this engine, the counterweight trebuchet, probably with a winch, and load it with a missile and lock it in place. This lifts and fixes the weight at the short end. Release the long end, the weight (on a pivot so it can fall straight) plunges, the long end flies round, the sling extends, multiplying the speed of the missile, and off it goes (Fig. 6).

The big ones, the ones with names like *War-wolf*, had beams fifteen and eighteen meters long and counterweights of hundreds of kilograms. They cast missiles of more than a hundred kilograms for hundreds of meters. They were not only more powerful but more accurate than any missile deliverer yet, as you would expect of a machine with a minimum of direct involvement of human muscles. A recent reconstruction in Denmark of a medium-sized trebuchet has grouped its shots in a six-meter square at a distance of 180 meters.[23]

Hobbyists and madmen in our time have constructed trebuchets and have flung grand pianos and automobiles goodly distances, confirmation of the immense utility these machines once

[23] The counterweight can be hinged or not hinged, propped or not propped. If you are interested, consult Les Eigenbrod, Vernard Foley, and Werner Soedel, "The Trebuchet," *Scientific American*, Vol. 273 (July 1995), 66–71.

Figure 6. A medium-sized counterweight trebuchet. Robert Payne-Gallway, *The Crossbow* (1903). By permission of the New York Public Library.

had in warfare.[24] In the fall of 1998, a somewhat more serious group from the United States and several European nations gathered at Urquhart Castle at Inverness, Scotland, to build two trebuchets to learn whether castle walls could be destroyed with such weapons. They cast missiles as heavy as three hundred pounds and proved that trebuchets can knock down walls. The name of the project was "The Highland Fling."[25]

The counterweight trebuchet enormously advanced the fortunes of attackers as compared to defenders. Chhin Chün, looking back from the fifteenth century, wrote,

> From the time when these trebuchets were first made, they were used for the besieging of cities, and there was never one

---

[24] Paul E. Chevedden et al., "The Trebuchet," *Scientific American*, Vol. 273 (July 1995), 67–71.

[25] Timber Framers Guild: Report on the Trebuchet Workshop; Timberframers Guild: Nova/WGBH Trebuchet Project.

which they did not break, nor was any ship not sunk by them when they were used against ships.[26]

This trebuchet spread rapidly because of its general military usefulness and because, in all probability, of its special usefulness to the Mongols, who in the 1200s were creating the biggest empire ever. They were mounted warriors, not engineers. They did not defend, but assaulted, and needed means to level walls. The Muslims may have invented the counterweight trebuchet; the Franks soon after may have been building the biggest yet; but it was the Mongols who needed them most and had the where-withal – prestige, money, posh military and bureaucratic appointments – to hire experts to build the biggest and best. They enlisted Persians, Syrians, and, according to Marco Polo, Franks such as himself and his brother Nicolo, as builders of trebuchets.[27]

The Mongols were utilizing the new engines extensively and with success by mid-thirteenth century, against, for instance, the Rus at the siege of Kiev in 1240[28] and against the Chinese at the siege of Hsian-yang in the 1270s. With victories there and elsewhere the Mongols won control over most of Eurasia and established a Pax Mongolica. This peace assured transcontinental traders and travelers of safety and even a degree of hospitality across a vaster area that had ever been so disposed before. During

[26] Joseph Needham, "China's Trebuchets, Manned and Counterweighted" in *On Pre-Modern Technology and Science, A Volume of Studies in Honor of Lynn White, Jr.,* eds. Bert S. Hall and Delno C. West (Malibu, CA: Undena Publications, 1976), 107–19.

[27] Lynn White, Jr., "The Crusades and the Technological Thrust of the West" in *War, Technology and Society in the Middle East,* eds. V. J. Parry and M. E. Yapp (London: Oxford University Press, 1975) 102–3; Joseph Needham, *Science and Civilisation in China, V. Chemistry and Chemical Technology, Part 7, Military Technology; The Gunpowder Epic* (Cambridge: Cambridge University Press, 1986), 572–3.

[28] Janet Martin, *Medieval Russia, 980–1584* (Cambridge: Cambridge University Press, 1996), 139, 140.

the few decades of the Pax, new ideas and inventions and what-have-you flowed across the Hearthland as never before: paper, printing, the counterweight trebuchet.

If desired, trebuchets could heave missiles other than boulders. No package that might torment or dispatch the enemy was unworthy of launching. The Mongols threw firebombs over the walls of Hsian-yang and victims of the Black Death over the walls of Caffa on the Crimean coast. This may have provided the link via Genoese merchants and sailors between the pandemic in Asia and that in Western Europe in 1347.[29]

The Chinese were so impressed with trebuchets that some of the Taoists came to believe that the great engines had their own tutelary deity. Wang I wrote of of their missiles and the prowess of their makers:

> Through wind and clouds they ride upon their way,
> Like shooting stars they thunder through space –
> Over the walls, crash! Down go temples and halls,
> And all the people are thrown into confusion.
> Thus the height of technique achieves the height of victory.[30]

These engines were, until the invention of gunpowder bombards, central to the hopes and fears of all in the Hearthland who would besiege and were besieged. They were also big, complicated, and difficult to adjust for even minimal effectiveness, and were not made by nobles, merchants, or peasants taking time off from their regular occupations. For instance, the construction of King Edward I. of England's giant trebuchet *War-wolf* required

[29] Robert S. Guttfried, *The Black Death: Natural and Human Disaster in Medieval Europe* (New York: Free Press, 1983), 36–7.
[30] Needham, "China's Trebuchets," in *On Pre-Modern Technology and Science*, 119.
[31] Payne-Gallwey, *Crossbow*, 261.

fifty carpenters and, more to the point, five foremen.[31] Such experts may qualify as the first specialists in military hardware to be so highly esteemed that they could peddle their skills to societies right across the map, like the German rocketeers after World War II. When the Count of Hainault asked one such expert, almost certainly a commoner, to make trebuchets for the siege of Lille in 1297, he addressed him as his "very dear master of engines."[32]

There was no decline in the use of trebuchets in Europe until after 1380, and in 1475–76 at the siege of Burgos they were heaving away right alongside the new gunpowder bombards. They even figured in the first siege of the Old World's invasion of the New. Hernán Cortés, running short of gunpowder, had a trebuchet built for his siege of Tenochtitlán (Mexico City) in 1521. It heaved its missile quite nearly straight up, which returned quite nearly straight back. Cortés had it dismantled.[33] Trebuchets are simple in principle, but not in practice, as today's hobbyists might keep in mind.

∗ ∗ ∗

Throwing, be it simply the delivery of a rock by hand or a whole dead horse via trebuchet, represented only one of humanity's two favorite ways to effect change at a distance. The other is fire. Humans have dreamed of combining the two from the first time an angry hominid snatched a burning brand from a campfire and threw it at the cause of his wrath, or in all innocence swung a torch up into the night sky simply to see it streak and spark.

---

[32] Needham and Yates, *Science and Civilisation in China*, 218, 222; *The Travels of Marco Polo, Venetian*, trans. Jon Corbino (Garden City: Doubleday & Co., 1948), 217; Needham, "China's Trebuchets, Manned and Counterweighted," 118; Contamine, *War in the Middle Ages*, 194.

[33] Phillipe Contamine, *War in the Middle Ages* (Barnes and Noble, 1998), 194–6; *"We People Here: Nahuatl Accounts of the Conquest of Mexico"* James Lockhart, trans. and ed., in *Reportorium Columbianum*, Vol. 2 (Berkeley: University of California Press, 1993), 230–1.

Humans doubtlessly used burning arrows, a wicked weapon in a world with wicker huts and thatched roofs, long before we have any written or artistic records. Then the size of incendiary missiles increased with the height of walls and the bulk of armies. Besiegers were already pitching firepots into towns in the ninth century B.C.E., according to Assyrian bas-reliefs, and defenders were throwing fire right back. Sun Tzu, who wrote *Ping-fa*, the first known military treatise, in the fourth century B.C.E., during what the Chinese call the Warring States period, recommends five uses of fire in battle, including hurling.[34]

Flaming missiles of straw and wood were insufficiently destructive and murderous to content humanity for long. They bounced off and fell away from walls and towers and were easily extinguished by water. What was wanted was something that would burn fiercely, adhere stubbornly, and resist being put out with water. A third-century C.E. writer, Philostratus, mentions an incendiary oil made by melting down white worms of the river Hyphasis in India, an oil that, ignited, could not be put out, and which a local king used to burn walls and capture cities.[35]

Such combustibles could be obtained in greater quantities from plants (e.g., pitch from pine trees), and there were more generous sources, stores of ancient solar energy – naptha, bitumen, and other kinds of petroleum – oozing from bedrock, particularly in what we call the Middle East today. These burned like hellfire, and with a few supplements would stick like honey; throwing water on their flames served not to extinguish them but to spread

[34] Stockholm International Peace Research Institute, *Incendiary Weapons* (Cambridge: MIT Press, 1975), 15; J. R. Partington, *A History of Greek Fire and Gunpowder* (New York: W. Heffner and Sons, 1960), 1, Sun Tzu, *The Art of War*, trans. Lionel Giles (The Internet Classics Archive by Daniel C. Stevenson, Web Atomics), Chapter 12.

[35] Lynn Thorndike, *A History of Magic and Experimental Science during the First Thirteen Centuries of Our Era* (New York: Macmillan, 1929), Vol. 1, 256–7.

them. At Somosata on the Euphrates there was a pool of a substance reputed to burn under water.[36]

Such substances could be wonderfully useful – if the enemy would stay in one spot to have petroleum poured on him and if he were cooperative in the matter of being ignited. An Arab chronicler provides us with one such example. At the end of the twelfth century during the Muslim siege of Acre, a Crusader capital, the attackers threw pots of naptha and similar combustibles against one of the Christians' towers. Nothing happened because the pots were unlighted and without fuses. The Christians, cheered by this display of their enemies' incompetency, climbed back into the tower. *Then* the Arabs threw a burning pot. The tower exploded into flame and its defenders were consumed.[37]

But enemies, even dull-minded Franks, would seldom be that cooperative. What was needed was a practical means of throwing actual fire. During the Peloponnesian War the Boeotians besieging Delium had tried to project flames or at least hot gases. They constructed a contraption consisting of a large wooden tube mated to a bellows and a caldron filled with the burning coals, sulphur, and pitch. They brought the machine right up to Delium, pumped the bellows, and blew a huge flame from the caldron against the wall. The defenders abandoned their positions and while they were in disarray the Boeotians stormed the wall and won the city.[38] Congratulations to them, but the range of their incendiary weapon could have been no more than a few meters and their enemies conveniently incompetent.

The first impresarios of incendiary warfare were the Byzantines. The name of their weapon, bestowed by the Crusaders, was Greek

---

[36] Partington, *History of Greek Fire*, 3.

[37] Stockholm International Peace Research Institute, *Incendiary Weapons*, 17; Partington, *History of Greek Fire*, 3.

[38] *Thucydides: The Peloponnesian War*, trans. Rex Warner (Harmondsworth: Penguin Books, 1985), 325.

Fire. One legend has it that the Greeks invented it during the siege of Troy. Not true. Another had it that, circa 300 C.E., a bellicose angel revealed its formula to Constantine the Great, the first Christian emperor of the Roman empire. Not true, either, but those whose capital was named Constantinople, the Byzantine Christians, were the first to use it. The date was probably some time in the seventh century C.E.

Greek Fire was a napalm-like liquid or gel that could be delivered in small packages such as hand grenades or in big ones in tubs via trebuchets, or pumped, burning, out of tubes, big and small. It stuck to whatever it hit, flammable or not, and water did not put it out. It would even burn on water and, according to some accounts, ignited on contact with water. It must have consisted of some sort of distilled petroleum plus one or more ingredients to make it stick and just possibly saltpeter to intensify the combustion. The record has it that only vinegar, sand, or urine would extinguish it. That nugget of information doesn't help us at all with its formula.[39]

Greek Fire figured importantly in the Byzantines' successes against the Muslims and others on land and especially at sea. The Greeks delivered the flaming substance, probably in spurts with some sort of a syringe pump, onto and into enemy vessels through flexible hoses in the mouths of ferocious lions and monsters cast of metal. Their enemies, wrote the Byzantine chronicler Theophanes, "shivered in terror, recognizing how strong the liquid fire was."[40]

[39] Partington, *History of Greek Fire*, 28; Christine de Pizan, *The Book of Deeds of Arms and of Chivalrey*, trans. Summer Willard (University Park: Pennsylvania University Press, 1999), 141; Needham, "China's Trebuchets," in *On Pre-Modern Technology and Science*, 111; Alex Roland, "Secrecy, Technology, and War: Greek Fire and the Defense of Byzantium, 678–1204," *Technology and Culture*, Vol. 33 (October 1992), 655–9.
[40] Partington, *History of Greek Fire*, 14–20.

The historian, Geoffrey de Villehardouin, a twelfth-century Frank who was a target for Greek Fire delivered via trebuchet, described it as seeming "like a dragon flying through the air." (The noise he credited to the projectile, "like that of a thunderbolt," suggests rocketry, but the date is too early. The roar must have been produced by the rapid flight through the air of the fiercely burning missile.)

The Byzantines tried to keep the formula for Greek Fire secret, but petroleum and such were widely available geographically then as now, and the Greeks' rivals and enemies were far from being chemically incompetent. By the year 1000 the Chinese had a device with a double action pump that emitted a steady stream of fire. The Muslims used incendiary weapons like Greek Fire in every battle with the Crusaders after the middle decades of the twelfth century. A hundred years later the Mongols with their giant trebuchets were throwing firebombs, probably of naptha, possibly of some substance even more explosively flammable.

In the 1200s armies were throwing Greek Fire or something like it in battle and siege in all the major regions of the Hearthland except laggard western Europe. Oddly, though, the first masters of the practice, the Byzantines, seldom mentioned Greek Fire after 1000, and there is no evidence of their using it, at least not under that name, after 1200.[41] The explanation cannot be that their interest in projectile fire technology decreased as their enemies' use of it increased. It may be that the precise formula, reserved to the emperor and his closest associates, was killed off in one of the many

[41] Partington, *History of Greek Fire*, 22, 28; Needham, "China's Trebuchets" in *On Pre-Modern Technology and Science*, 111; Robert Temple, *The Genius of China: 3,000 Years of Science, Discovery, and Inventions* (New York: Simon and Schuster, 1986), 229; W. Y. Carman, *A History of Firearms from the Earliest Times to 1914* (London: Routledge and Kegan Paul Ltd., 1955), 6; Peter Pentz, "A Medieval Workshop for Producing 'Greek Fire' Grenades," *Antiquity*, Vol. 62 (March 1988), 92.

palace coups. It may be that after a while everyone had it or something like it, so it wasn't flaunted as a secret weapon any more.[42]

Or perhaps something new was coming along that rendered Greek Fire obsolescent. The arms race with which we in our time are unpleasantly familiar was accelerating. Something new, dreadful, launchable, and flammable was bound to appear. Indeed, it already had done so, and no spot on the habitable surface of the earth would be beyond its influence. It was gunpowder.

[42] Alex Roland, "Secrecy Technology, and War: Greek Fire and the Defense of Byzantium, 678–1204," *Technology and Culture*, Vol. 33 (October 1992), 662, 663–5, 666–70.

The Second Acceleration:
Gunpowder

*I*n the first half-millennium C.E. centralized polities existed across the Hearthland, but there were broad expanses where their actual power did not reach, and the centers were in only intermittent contact with each other: Beijing had little or no knowledge or interest in Rome or vice versa. Hearthland societies had no more than fleeting contact with those of sub-Saharan Africa and northern Eurasia, and not even that with the peoples of America and Oceania. The Hearthland circa 500 C.E. was a lineup of batteries sitting alone and connected in series with faulty wiring.

The centripetal tendency was slow for many more reasons than we have space for here. To offer one pertinent to our special inquiry, projectile technology was still too primitive to fill the defensive and offensive needs of more ambitious merchants, missionaries, and soldiers. These centripetalists, mired in general resistance to innovation and often distrusted and even hated, needed improved means of defense and attack. They needed a much better way to kill at a distance and, thereby, to inspire

93

admiration, to intimidate, to subjugate, and to tamp civilization down the throats of people who otherwise would go on with their lives of provinciality and sleepy convention.

The situation changed in the centuries adjoining 1000 C.E. as the connections between the Hearthland batteries began to work better. Islam arose and spread and Arabic became the language of elites from Spain to central Asia. Muslim sailors swept east and west with the monsoons across the Indian Ocean and beyond. Slavers herded their cogitative wares across Eurasia and Africa, east and west, north and south. Merchants traversed the Silk Road: in 1261, *mirabile dictu*, Scandinavian traders, bizarrely blond and blue-eyed, showed up in the Mongol court.[1] Professional travelers – Marco Polo and Ibn Battuta the most famous, but not the first nor last – sought out the exotic and, once back home, told eager audiences of what they had seen. New means of killing at a distance – the crossbow, the trebuchet, Greek Fire, gunpowder – ran like quicksilver from one end of the Hearthland to the other. Of these the most important was the newest, gunpowder.

---

[1] Joseph Needham, *Science and Civilisation in China*, Vol. 5, Pt. 7, *Military Technology: The Gunpowder Epic* (Cambridge: Cambridge University Press, 1986), 568–79; Janet L. Abu-Lughod, *Before European Hegemony: The World System A.D. 1250–1350.* (New York: Oxford University Press, 1989), 34 and passim.

SIX

The Chinese Elixir

The black dragon lobbed over an egg-shaped thing
Fully the size of a peck measure it was. And it burst, and
a dragon flew out with peals of thunder rolling. In the
air it was like a blazing and flashing fire. The first bang
was like the dividing of chaos in two, As if mountains
and rivers were all turned upside down...

> Chang Hsien, "Thieh Phao Hsing" (c. 1341)[1]

Grape rattles on the roofs of the houses and in the
fields; cannon balls howl over us, and plough the air in
all directions, and soon there is the frequent whistling
of musket balls.

> Karl von Clausewitz, *On War* (1833)[2]

---

[1] Joseph Needham, *Science and Civilisation in China,* Vol. 5, Pt. 7, *Military Technology; The Gunpowder Epic* (Cambridge: Cambridge University Press, 1986), 270.
[2] Carl von Clausewitz, *On War,* trans. J. J. Graham (Ware, U. K.: Wordsworth Editions, 1997), 61.

Gunpowder was in its origin not a product of war nor did it begin as an incendiary per se. It swam up out of simmering stew of primordial mystical beliefs and seems to have begun as an elixir, of all things. All the way across the Hearthland, alchemists, who are to chemists as astrologists are to astronomers, were trying to discern the secret nature of reality by investigating the essences and relationships of various materials, especially such peculiar ones as mercury, a liquid metal, and sulphur, a stone that would burn. The Chinese Taoist alchemists conducted an examination of such substances so prolonged and so systematic that it was bound to turn up something important.[3]

By the end the first millennium C.E. they were well acquainted with materials containing saltpeter (potassium nitrate), a substance formed by the decomposition of organic matter. (It often appears as a whitish bloom on cellar walls.) Saltpeter is a peculiar substance indeed. It does not merely combine with the oxygen in the air, but supplies oxygen itself – that is, it will burn furiously and insist that others do also under the most inardent circumstances.

Saltpeter was, according to Taoists, the prince of gunpowder, and other ingredients, sulphur and charcoal, its ministers. Such was the case because, as they expressed it, saltpeter expands *vertically,* while sulphur, for instance, expands *horizontally.*[4] This seems to mean that saltpeter is *very* volatile and the other two are not. Late in the first millennium C.E. a volume entitled *Classified Essentials of the Mysterious Tao of the True Origins of Thing* warned that experiments in heating mixtures of saltpeter, sulphur, arsenic, and honey had ended in disaster: "Hands and faces have

---

[3] Joseph Needham, *Science and Civilisation in China*, Vol. 5, Pt. 7, 5; Joseph Needham, "Gunpowder as the Fourth Power, East and West," Occasional Papers' Series No. 3, East Asian History of Science Foundation, Hong Kong University Press, 1985, 29.

[4] Needham, *Science and Civilisation in China*, Vol. 5, Pt. 7, 364.

been burnt, and even the whole house where they were working burned down."[5] Surely such a substance would be good for ringworm, would improve health in general, and might even prolong life indefinitely.[6]

The crucial factor in how fast gunpowder burns is the proportion of saltpeter to the other ingredients. The sulphur and charcoal participate in combustion, but it is the saltpeter that is crucial. If the mixture includes a goodly amount of saltpeter, it will burn rapidly. If it includes 75 percent saltpeter, it will burn so rapidly as to produce in an instant 3,000 times its bulk in gas – an explosion.[7]

It was inevitable that something that likely to ignite and throw things around would be utilized for war in the Hearthland, where enemies were pitching boulders and squirting Greek Fire at each other. This innovation was especially likely among the Song Chinese, vigorous, clever, and needful of means to defend themselves from each other and nomad threats on the frontier.

It may have been China's bamboo that accustomed the earliest gunpowder engineers to the idea that explosions are survivable and even useful. Throw a stalk of bamboo on the fire and the air enclosed between the septa will expand explosively with a loud bang. The Chinese had been playing with such explosions for many generations before gunpowder, and the transition from bamboo to firecrackers was easy. By the thirteenth century at the latest the Chinese New Year's Eves were as noisy and smoky as they are today.[8]

Nailing down an exact date for the first explosive bomb is impossible. That task defied even the awesome skills and energy of the University of Cambridge sinophile and historian of science Joseph Needham. When were "thunderclap bombs" succeeded by "heaven-

---

[5] Needham, *Science and Civilisation in China*, Vol. 5, Pt. 7, 112.
[6] Needham, *Science and Civilisation in China*, Vol. 5, Pt. 7, 111–17.
[7] Robert Temple, *Genius of China: 300 Years of Science, Discovery, and Inventions* (New York: Simon and Schuster, 1986), 228–9.
[8] Needham, *Science and Civilisation in China*, Vol. 5, Pt. 7, 128, 132, 134.

shaking thunder-crash bombs" and what exactly was the difference between them?[9] Were they bombs, as we use the word, at all or were they chiefly utilized and effective as noisemakers? The battlefield was relatively quiet when gunpowder arrived, and noise in itself could be a weapon. Muslims, when they first obtained gunpowder, would send out avant-gardes of horses and horsemen in fireproof garb hung with skeins of firecrackers to stampede opponents.[10]

Was the "bone-burning and bruising fire-oil magic bomb" a real bomb? It had a gunpowder core to facilitate the distribution of the rest of this package's contents, a Satanic porridge of urine, feces, scallion juice, iron pellets, and broken porcelain packed in a purposely weak casing. A contemporary proclaimed that even birds in the air could not escape its effects, which would seem likely, but that does not make it an actual bomb.[11]

As the decades passed, the proportion of saltpeter kept creeping up, the casing of the gunpowder, often of thick layers of paper and finally of metal, grew tighter and stronger. No later than the thirteenth century and probably earlier, the Chinese were flinging gunpowder grenades by hand and gunpowder bombs by trebuchet. Modern warfare was under way and the peoples of the Hearthland had gained the power to conquer the rest of the world; and such hecatombs of Verdun and Stalingrad were perhaps inevitable.[12]

The devising of ways to use the expansion of gunpowder's gases to propel whole missiles as well as scatter their contents was also Chinese in its beginnings. The Chinese familiarity with bamboo may have been significant in this innovation too. They, for whom the very strong though hollow bamboo was an everyday

[9] Needham, *Science and Civilisation in China*, Vol. 5, Pt. 7, 170–3, 180–1.
[10] Ahmad Y. al-Hassan and Donald R. Hill, *Islamic Technology, An Illustrated History* (Cambridge: Cambridge University Press, 1986), 119–20.
[11] Needham, *Science and Civilisation in China*, Vol. 5, Pt. 7, 170–3, 180–1.
[12] Needham, *Science and Civilisation in China*, Vol. 5, Pt. 7, 163–79.

material, were pre-adapted to think in terms of tubes.[13] Guns are tubes that confine the gases of explosions behind a missile in order to force it out of the muzzle at a high velocity.

The Chinese tried all manner of missile delivery systems, catapults and trebuchets and others, even live birds and oxen.[14] None of these pointed the Chinese down the path to guns until the invention in the 900s of something Joseph Needham has translated into English as the fire-lance. It was a tube closed at one end and open at the other loaded with a gunpowder mixture with more sulphur and charcoal than saltpeter. The tube, at first probably of bamboo and in time of metal, was fastened to a lance beside the spearhead with the open end pointing outward. The fire-lance was not supposed to explode or, in its first versions, to project missiles. It was in purpose like a handheld Greek fire pump, a sort of five-minute flame thrower, effective against infantry and cavalry and particularly useful to soldiers defending fortress or city walls against assault from below.

At first the fire-lance spewed nothing but flame. Then someone realized that the fire-lance had expulsive power and began to add sand, irritants, and poisons to the gunpowder, then broken crockery, metal bits, and eventually arrows, often several at a time. Innovators enlarged some of the fire-lances until they sat on their own carriages, strengthened their tubes, and increased the proportion of saltpeter in the propellant. When the diameter of the missile (or missiles) grew so great relative to the diameter of the tube as to assure that the hot gases would not escape until they thrust the projectile or projectiles out of the barrel (a more accurate word than tube by this time) at a high velocity – when the primary purpose of the device had advanced from projecting fire to projecting missiles – then this weapon had become a gun. That was certainly no later than the beginning of the

---

[13] Needham, "Gunpowdeer as the Fourth Power, East and West," 8.
[14] Needham, *Science and Civilisation in China*, Vol. 5, Pt. 7, 210–15.

Figure 7. A hand cannon, c. 1400, ancestor of the harquebus and musket. Niedersachsiste Staatsund Universitatsbibliothek, Gottingen.

fourteenth century.[15] By the middle of the next century such weapons were standard in the armies of China and, barely a step behind, of many other armies of the Hearthland (Fig. 7).

The explosive gases of burning gunpowder can be utilized to propel objects away – bullets, cannon balls, bombs – or to propel the object that contains the explosion. The former operation is that of the gun or cannon. The latter is that of the rocket. The early wielders of fire-lances certainly felt the recoil, that is, the rocket effect, of their devices. For every action there is an equal and opposite reaction, as Sir Isaac Newton codified into a law of nature some hundreds of years later.

In the twelfth century the Chinese improved the fire arrow, which everyone had been shooting with bows for millennia, by fix-

[15] Needham, *Science and Civilisation in China*, Vol. 5, Pt. 7, 220–1, 223, 229, 231, 247–8, 254, 284, 288–9, 299–304; Arnold Pacey, *Technology in World Civilization* (Cambridge: MIT Press, 1990), 47.

ing to it small containers of gunpowder. The saltpeter prevented the rapid flight through the air from blowing the fire out, but arrows were not self-propelling missiles. In fact, arrows with packages on board were heavier and blunter and did not fly as fast or far as standard arrows, especially if the package were burning and sputtering and creating thrust backwards. That impediment provoked experimentation.

The Chinese could not have failed to notice that sometimes the burning compartments of bamboo (sections closed off by septa at the ends) would not simply explode, but one septum would perforate first and the hot air escaping through the hole would send the bamboo whizzing wildly this way and that. That inspired someone somewhere to cut a hole in one end of a compartment of bamboo, stuff gunpowder with a subdetonation proportion of saltpeter inside, and light it. Then he had to jump out of the way, having constructed and ignited the first fireworks rocket. In 1264 these unguided missiles – they were called ground-rats or fire-rats – made their debut in the imperial court at a feast and entertainment for the Empress Kung Sheng. She was not amused, but gathered her skirts around her in the fashion of Victorian ladies threatened by mice and halted the feast.[16]

Fire-rats had already been used in battle. There was something called a watermelon bomb, which was especially effective for defending city walls. It contained gunpowder to scatter the rest of the contents: hundreds of caltrops (sort of multispiked thumbtacks for piercing feet) and scores of fire-rats to ignite and scurry about and frighten the enemy and his horses.[17]

Some time during these years Chinese archers realized that fastening a tiny fire-lance backwards on an arrow, so it pointed toward the bowman rather than the enemy, greatly increased the velocity and range of the missile (Fig. 8). It might also scorch the

[16] Needham, *Science and Civilisation in China*, Vol. 5, Pt. 7, 135
[17] Needham, *Science and Civilisation in China*, Vol. 5, Pt. 7, 474.

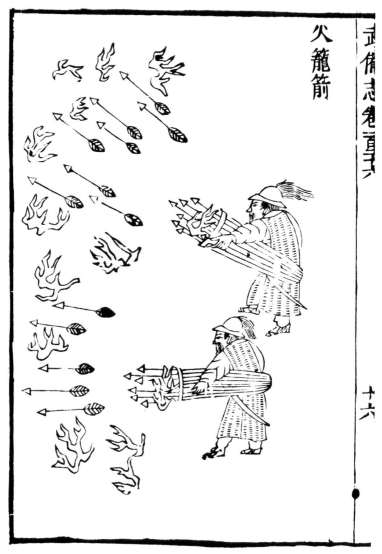

火籠箭

武備志卷百三十六

十六

Figure 8. Chinese basketwork rocket launchers. Needham, *Science and Civilisation in China*, Vol 5, Part 7.

bowman, but that problem could be solved with a short fuse to assure that the gunpowder would not ignite until the arrow was on its way. Or, better, one could dispense with the bow completely and launch the arrow from its own platform – as a rocket, we would say. Stand to one side, light the powder packet, and away the arrow would go. Weapons called "flying fire-lances," rockets in all probability, may have been used in combat as early as 1200.[18]

Improvements came in a rush. The Chinese and their enemies learned that the cylinder of burning gunpowder that drove the missile should have a hollow center so the fuel would burn evenly and the rocket would fly straight. They discovered that narrowing the exit port of the rocket so as to increase the backwards velocity of the escaping hot gases would increase the forward velocity of the missile. Soon flights of five hundred meters and more became standard. The rockets were very inaccurate, but when fired from racks by the score, by the hundreds, could devastate cities or, alternatively, throw besieging forces into chaos.[19]

The Chinese had taken centuries to develop gunpowder weapons, but it took no more than a few decades, perhaps only years during the Pax Mongolica, for the knowledge of how to make them to sweep the full length of the Hearthland. That knowledge was carried by a new class, the masters of the new military technology. Gunpowder weapons required true professionals to manufacture and to train others to use them. These specialists became indispensable and therefore mobile across borders of all kinds.

---

[18] Needham, *Science and Civilisation in China*, Vol. 5, Pt. 7, 477–9; Jixing Pan, "The Origin of Rockets in China" in *Gunpowder: The History of an International Technology*, ed. Brenda J. Buchanan (Bath: Bath University Press, 1996), 27–8.
[19] Needham, *Science and Civilisation in China*, Vol. 5, Pt. 7, 472–95.

To cite one early instance, by 1300 or so Mongol converts to Islam in northwest India were throwing fiery, probably gunpowder, missiles with bows and traction trebuchet. A few of these Neo-Muslims, according to Amir Khusrau, even "turned their faces from the Sun of Islam and joined the Saturnians," the Hindus.[20]

More and more people have since then become addicted to gunpowder and its successors, such as gun cotton, TNT, and nuclear bombs, because of our conviction that if we are inferior to others in firepower, we will be bullied and even conquered. That is an often but not universally valid argument, and should, one would think, be liable in specific instances to reasoned counterargument. But there is more to our addiction to explosives than reason. We love them for themselves, for their spectacle, the joy and terror they produce.

In 1776 Benjamin Franklin, worried that the American rebels would not have enough gunpowder, played with the thought that they might have to resort to bows and arrows: "good weapons, not wisely laid aside." He pointed to the fact that an archer's accuracy was at least as good as a musketeer's, and that he could discharge four arrows in the time it took to load and fire one bullet. Gunpowder produced smoke, obscuring the battlefield; arrows didn't. A man lightly wounded with a musket ball might continue to fight, but, "an arrow striking any part of as man puts him *hors du combat* till it is extracted." Last and most important: "Bows and arrows are more easily provided everywhere than muskets and ammunition."[21]

If as wise a man as Franklin could entertain such retrogressive sentiments five hundred years into the gunpowder era, by which time small arms usually worked on even rainy days and cannon

---

[20] Iqtidar Alam Khan, "Coming of Gunpowder to the Islamic World and North India: Spotlight on the Role of the Mongols," *Journal of Asian History*, Vol. 30 (Spring 1996), 41–5.

[21] Benjamin Franklin, *Works of Benjamin Franklin* (Boston: 1839), Vol. 8, 169–70.

rarely blew up in cannoneers' faces, then how is it that supposedly sensible men were, as we shall see in the next chapter, so eager to adopt gunpowder weapons back when the opposite was true?

Because, simply, we adore boom and flash, which extends to the way we celebrate as well as fight. In the year 1999, including purchases for the New Year's Eve celebration of the new millennium, the rich of this world and, yes, the poor, too, cast away for no lasting advantage whatsoever immense sums on fireworks. The United States alone vaporized 156.9 million pounds of fireworks.[22] Humans glory in detonation. It is glamorous.

Detonation taps humanity's primordial fascination with fire and thunderclap. It also provides an outlet for the frenzy that sets our younger children and older drunks to aimless slinging of stones, food, excrement, of whatever can be thrown that will make a satisfying mess. With detonation we achieve such self-expression colossally.

For evidence of this we turn to our experts on the yearnings with which our reason cannot cope and often doesn't even recognize. We must turn to the poets. In Book VI of "Paradise Lost" John Milton blames a pre-Adamite invention of gunpowder on his glamorous anti-hero, Satan. The poet indulges his suppressed infatuation with the great rebel and for havoc in general with a lurid description of the monstrous archangel's cannon:

> From those deep-throated Engines belcht, whose roar
> Embowell'd with outrageous noise the Air,
> And all her entrails tore, disgorging foul
> Thir devilish, chain'd Thunderbolts and Hail
> Of Iron Globes, which on the Victor Host
> Levell'd, with such impetuous fury smote,
> That whom they hit, none on thir feet might stand,
> Though standing else as Rocks, but down they fell
> By thousands, Angel on Arch-Angel roll'd...

[22] Personal communication from Julie Heckman, American Pyrotechnics Association.

Satan doesn't win, of course. Archangel Michael flings whole mountains in retaliation and God sends His Son to drive Satan and his legions out of the Heavens and into the abyss of Hell, cannon and all. But Milton predicts what he, of course, knows will come, a future in which gunpowder will figure:

> In future days, if Malice should abound,
> Some one intent on mischief, or inspir'd
> With dev'lish machination might devise
> Like instrument to plague the Sons of men
> For sin, on war and mutual slaughter bent.[23]

Every age after the first dissemination of gunpowder would have glamour weapons from the medieval bombard to the fifty-megaton hydrogen bomb.

---

[23] John Milton, *Paradise Lost, Paradise Regained, and Samson Agonistes* (Garden City, NY: International Collectors Library, 1969), 148, 150.

SEVEN

Gunpowder as a Centripetal Force

A single one of us can defeat your whole army. If you do not believe it, you may try, only please order your army to stop shooting with firearms.

An unnamed Mamluk emir,
prisoner to Selim the Grim, Ottoman Sultan,
after the battle of Marjdabik, 1516[1]

Humanity used gunpowder, which blows things apart, to compress communities together into empires and nations. The history of that process, is, in its details, a garter snake roil of wars, battles, subjugations, and intimidations that defies neat classification and consideration. Yet classify and consider we must because any attempt to understand the last millennium that omits gunpowder would be like an explanation of geology without volcanic action.

A useful way to approach the subject is to arrange societies in ascending order in accordance with the rapidity-cum-magnitude of the political effects of gunpowder on them. There are two vari-

---

[1] David Ayalon, *Gunpowder and Firearms in the Mamluk Kingdom* (London: Vallentine, Mitchell and Co., 1956), 94.

ables to consider about these societies: the velocity, moderate or abrupt, of their introductions to the new explosive, and the depth of the roots of their political and general cultural traditions resisting changes associated with the new weaponry.

We start with the slowest and least affected, at least immediately. We begin with China, where, as we have seen, Taoist alchemists were scorching themselves with saltpeter mixtures when Charlemagne ruled and then centuries more passed before the first guns and rockets. Gunpowder sizzled and sputtered for a long time before it exploded there and, therefore, its influence was relatively sedate in its emergence and mild for many generations.

There is no civilization more firmly rooted than that of the Chinese. It suffered multiple devastations, but few truly shattering and lasting interruptions. The Roman Empire crumbled and nothing better than cheap knockoffs ever rose in western Europe to replace it. Chinese dynasties fell to internal revolt and invasion time and again, then similar dynasties sprouted on their graves and the empire structure endured.

The tradition of obedience to an emperor and of deference to a mandarin bureaucracy was old when gunpowder weaponry appeared. In the following millennium the Chinese made free use of it several times over to settle the question of which dynasty possessed the Mandate of Heaven, and then settled back to run along deep and ancient grooves.

In the seventeenth century the Manchus encroached from the north, and they and the Ming dynasty's armies, with primeval guns and rockets blazing, fought until the invaders took over as the Qing dynasty. Then the Manchus gratefully and gracefully succumbed to being rendered culturally Chinese and turned their attention to more important matters than improving projectile weaponry.

There was one occasion, an anomalous but instructive one, in that century when a Qing emperor thought it might to advisable to update his ordnance. A practical man, he summoned not Chinese technicians, but resident Europeans, Jesuit missionaries.

The Emperor ordered Father Ferdinand Verbiest, who had been providing excellent bronze astronomical instruments, to make cannon for him. Verbiest tried to refuse, promising to pray for His Majesty's success, but begging him for "leave not to concern himself with the warfare of this World."[2] The Emperor was not so pleased, and Verbiest restored and improved 300 old big cannon and cast 132 smaller pieces. He inscribed on each the name of a saint and the sign of Jesus. He also provided the Chinese with a book in their language on cannons, which they mislaid.[3] Their attention reverted to traditional concerns and they were still using some cannon of the Jesuit's design when called back to the subject by the booming of bigger and better British cannon in the Opium Wars two centuries later.[4]

Gunpowder's debut among the Japanese as a means of inflicting death and destruction was more abrupt than among the Chinese (though less so than among other peoples, as we shall see), and fueled sweeping but not profound changes among them. In 1543 the Japanese had, like the Chinese, an emperor, but one without power, and were embroiled in political turmoil when Portuguese adventurers arrived

[2] Joseph Needham, *Science and Civilisation in China*, Vol. 5, Pt. 7, *Military Technology: The Gunpowder Epic* (Cambridge: Cambridge University Press, 1986), 395.

[3] Carlo M. Cipolla, *Guns, Sails, and Empires* (New York: Pantheon Books, 1965), 115.

[4] Jeanna Waley-Cohen, "China and Western Technology in the Late Eighteenth Century" in *Technology and European Overseas Enterprise: Diffusion, Adaption and Adoption,* ed. Michael Adas (Brookfield, VT: Variorum, 1996), 405.

on a Chinese junk with harquebuses. The Japanese were currently making little use of gunpowder, but they, like everyone else in eastern Asia, had known about it for generations. It came as a new and impressive weapon, but not as a thunderbolt from out of the blue. They seized on it to lift themselves out of chaos.

Within a few years their swordmakers, perhaps the best metalsmiths in the world, were making harquebuses and light cannon. It would be these, not bombards, that would have prime influence on the course of history in Japan.[5] Their harquebuses were bigger in caliber and had more dependable trigger mechanisms than the European ones, and little cowls to protect the match from rain and conceal its glow at night. Oda Nobunga, a centralizer, ordered 500 for his army in 1549. His greatest triumph, the battle at Nagashino a quarter-century later, was decided by the withering firepower of his infantry. They fought in three ranks, firing in rotation, a solution to the problem of how long it took to load gunpowder weapons that the Japanese devised well before the Europeans.

Nobunga's soldiers, had they been familiar with Michel de Montaigne's essays, written contemporaneously with their efforts, might have been charmed by the Frenchman's appraisal of handheld firearms as being so effective that soldiers would soon be dragging "off to war enclosed in little forts such as those which the Ancients made their elephants carry."[6]

Nobunga, murdered in 1582, never saw the fruition of his plans for Japan. It was Toyotomi Hideyoshi – ex-farmer, crafty statesman, and tactical genius – who accomplished the unification of Japan and

<hr />

[5] C. R. Boxer, "Notes on Early European Military Influence in Japan, 1543–1853," in *Warfare and Empires: Contact and Conflict between European and Non-European Military and Maritime Forces and Cultures,* ed. Douglas M. Peers (Ashgate, Aldershot, UK: Variorum, 1997), 113, 114.

[6] Michel de Montaigne, *The Complete Essays,* trans. M. A. Screech (London: Penguin Books, 1987), 454.

the elevation of the emperor's status. He did so with the same means favored by Nobunga, massed infantry with firearms.[7]

But Japanese society remained in a perilous state. The *daimyo*, the lords, retained their own armed forces and gunpowder weaponry. The proud and quick-tempered samurai and even many peasants were still in possession of firearms and perhaps ready to renew violence. Portuguese and other strangers in oddly rigged vessels were prowling Japan's coastal waters and peddling their wares in its ports. A bizarre religion, Christianity, swept inland and won converts by the thousands. The Japanese seemed to have attained peace just as their society was transmogrifying into something unlikely to be properly Nipponese.

Hideyoshi turned Japan down a path, along which his successors continued, that transformed it from the country in eastern Asia that had been most open to outside influence into what outsiders called the Hermit Kingdom. Japan rejected nearly all contact with foreigners, ejected or executed Christian missionaries, and gave native Christians the choice of death or apostasy.

Even so, with thousands still in possession of firearms, the threat to Japanese stability lingered. Hideyoshi and his successors called in guns to be melted down for a huge statue of Buddha, restricted gun manufacturing to a shrinking number of smiths, encouraged the samurai's devotion to the sword and contempt for the gun, and rid Japan of all but a very few firearms. After the suppression of the Shimabara rebellion in 1637, a peasant and Christian uprising, Japanese soldiers made little use of firearms for two hundred years. Many of the samu-

[7] Asao Naohiro, "The Sixteenth Century Unification," in *The Cambridge History of Japan*, Vol. 4, *Early Modern Japan*, ed. John Whitney Hall (Cambridge: Cambridge University Press, 1991), 45, 53–4; Noel Perrin, *Giving Up the Gun: Japan's Reversion to the Sword, 1543–1879* (Boulder: Shambhala, 1980), 5–6, 8, 17 19.

rai warriors became bureaucrats who wore swords for emblematic purposes.[8]

Japan's rulers had picked up the gun to achieve some degree of political centralization, and then, in hopes of preserving just that, threw it back down. Their isolation lasted two centuries, until the American, Commodore Matthew Perry, sailed into Edo Bay in the 1850s with cannon big enough to have used Japanese cannon as missiles. In the world that gunpowder made, a society could delay, but not forever abstain from, participation in the gunpowder competition.

* * *

Gunpowder weaponry multiplied the war-waging capabilities of east Asians, but did not alter their political scene as radically as it did in the rest of the Hearthland. There, as always and everywhere, leaders emerged who aspired to be emperors, but they hadn't the proper tools to implement their ambitions. They often began their campaigns with victories in battle, but then the losers would skulk and scurry and slink behind city and castle walls. Sieges took time, months, even years, often longer than armies could be maintained in the field. The best of armies would succumb to hunger, infections, and disaffections. The centralizers needed something to break wall with, something to speed up the creation of empires, that is, cannon.

The first cannon that we have a good illustration of was a bit longer than a man is tall and pear-shaped rather than tubular in order to withstand the explosion in its breech. This famous illustration, from a European (the Milamete) manuscript dated 1326, shows a cannon loaded not with a cannonball but with a huge arrow (Fig. 9). (Such a projectile was not an oddity. In 1342

---

[8] Perrin, *Giving Up the Gun*, 26–7, 45–7, 65; Jurgis Elisonas, "Christianity and the Daimyo" in *Early Modern Japan*, 370.

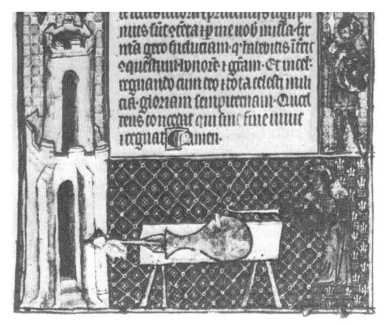

Figure 9. An early fourteenth-century illustration of a gunpowder cannon. Walter de Milamete manuscript, 1327. MS. 92 folio 70, The Library, Christ Church, Oxford.

French gun-founders were hired to make four hundred arrows with brass feathers to be fired by cannon.)[9]

The big cannon, the bombard – the wall-breaker – appeared in the last half of that century. Most of the early ones were not cast but built up like barrels. The gun-founders, often no more than blacksmiths, arranged bars of iron into a cylinder and then slid and pried iron rings, white hot, over and around the cylinder. As the rings cooled, they shrank, hugging the staves together. Only

[9] Needham, *Science and Civilisation in China*, Vol. 5, Pt. 7, 284–341; J. R. Partington, *A History of Greek Fire and Gunpowder* (New York: W. Heffner and Sons, 1960), 101; O. F. G. Hogg, *Artillery: Its Origin, Heyday and Decline* (London: Archon Books, 1970), 19, 32, 34, 67–8; Carlo M. Cipolla, *Guns, Sails, and Empires* (New York: Pantheon Books, 1965), opposite 96.

after a long while were craftsmen with experience in actual casting, bell-founders, hired to produce solid cannon, durable and less likely to burst and kill gunners.

Examples of bombard ordnance survive today in museums and castle courtyards. One of the biggest, Malik-i Maidan, cast in 1549, can be seen at Bijapur, India. It is more than four meters long, its bore seventy centimeters across. Its muzzle has the shape of a dragon with jaws open. One Mughal chronicler described such monsters as "wonderful locks for protecting the august edifice of the state and befitting keys for the door of conquest." Frederick the Great of Prussia was in his day equally enthused about cannon, which he called "the most respectable arguments of kings."[10]

It was with such tools that ambitious men built what historians Marshall G. S. Hodgson and William McNeill have called the Gunpowder Empires.[11] We will consider three, the Ottoman, Mughal, and Russian, each a major factor in world history, and then one more as a laboratory case.

The Ottomans Turks, by exercise of sword, composite bow, horsemanship, and statecraft, founded at the beginning of the 1300s a state in northwest Anatolia. From that center they began an expansion – east against the Seljuk Turks, south against the Mamluks, and west against the Byzantines – that made theirs one of the world's most powerful empires.

By the mid-1300s they dominated Asia Minor and were across the Dardanelles and into Europe. In the last half of that century they were utilizing artillery in battle and siege, especially in the Balkans, where they could buy firearms from the Italian city-states and hire Italian, Hungarian, and other local gunsmiths. In 1389

---

[10] M. K. Zaman, *Mughal Artillery* (Delhi: Vishal Printers, 1983), 11, 40; Hogg, *Artillery: Its Origin, Heyday and Decline*, dedication page.

[11] Marshall G. S. Hodgson, *The Gunpowder Empire and Modern Times* (Chicago: University of Chicago Press, 1974); William H. McNeill, *The Age of the Gunpowder Empires, 1450–1800* (Washington DC: American Historical Association, 1990).

they used firearms in defeating the Christian Serbs at Kossovo. "Gunfire boomed and the earth groaned," a Serbian monk recorded.[12] This was the earliest battle in which guns were employed that still, in the conflict of Muslims and Serbs in Kossovo, directly envenoms our lives.[13]

Ottoman armies won battle after battle, but there was a fish-bone in the Turkish throat: Constantinople. This, the Second Rome, the Christian capital of the Byzantine Empire, lay in the center of the Ottomans' Muslim empire. The Ottomans began their siege and their bombardment of this city the Turks called *Kizil Elma*, the Red Apple,[14] on April 6, 1453.

The city's advantages were the armed forces of its empire, on the wane in the sixteenth century, and the armies and navies of allies, often lukewarm in enthusiasm and tardy in arrival. The city was most dependably served by its location on a peninsula and by its immense walls. According to the Turkish Sultan, Mehemed II, "the empire of Constantinople is measured by her walls."

Urban, a Hungarian gun-founder and prime example of the new mobile military technical elite – a prefigure of Wernher von Braun – considered himself underpaid by his Christian masters and so took employment with Mehmed II for generous compensation. The first bombard he made for his new employer plunked a ball down on a Venetian ship in the Bosporus and sank it, an event more the result of Venetian bad luck than of the accuracy of any cannon of the age, but impressive all the same. Mehmed ordered

---

[12] Djurdjica Petrovic, "Firearms in the Balkans on the Eve of and after the Ottoman Conquests of the Fourteenth and Fifteenth Centuries" in *War, Technology and Society in the Middle East,* eds. V. J. Parry and M. E. Yapp (London: Oxford University Press, 1975), 172. 176, 179, 189.

[13] Needham, *Science and Civilisation in China,* Vol. 5, Pt. 7, 443; Cipolla, *Guns, Sails, and Empires,* 90; Petrovic, "Firearms in the Balkans" *War, Technology, and Society in the Middle East,* 172, 176, 179, 189.

[14] David Nicolle, *Armies of the Ottoman Turks, 1300–1774* (London: Osprey Publishing, 1983), 29.

Figure 10. A bombard such as used by Mehemed II in the siege of Constantinople, 1453.

another cannon, twice as big, the most gigantic cannon anywhere, the "Mahometta." It was nearly seven meters long and, according to tradition, made a noise so great that women within hearing had miscarriages. Its stone ball was over four hundred kilograms in weight. The gunpowder era had its first glamour weapon (Fig. 10).

The combatants, Turk and Greek, made use of all kinds of devices for casting stones and darts and also something called "liquid fire," but it was cannon, big and small, that dominated the battle. As the final assault on Constantinople began, the defenders of the city were looking down from walls that in many sectors were little more than moraines of rubble.[15] The Turks entered the city on May 29, 1453.[16]

Turkish example and sometimes even Turkish gun-founders (like Husain Khan, who in 1549 cast the Malik-i Maidan bombard

---

[15] Needham, *Science and Civilisation in China*, Vol. 5, Pt. 7, 368.

[16] Needham, *Science and Civilisation in China*, Vol. 5, Pt. 7, 366–8; Cipolla, *Guns, Sails, and Empires*, 93–4; Nicolle, *Armies of the Ottoman Turks*, 29–30; Edward Gibbon, *The Decline and Fall of the Roman Empire* (Chicago: Encyclopedia Britannica, 192), II, 546–7; Steven Runciman, *The Fall of Constantinople, 1453* (Cambridge: Cambridge University Press, 1990), 77–8, 97, 112, 136.

previously mentioned, spread gunpowder technology throughout the lands of Islam and as far as Sumatra. Their best pupils were perhaps the Mughals, who created an empire in India. Babur, the first of their emperors, won his initial triumph in 1526 at the battle of Panipat. The army of the enemy, the Sultan of Delhi, was bigger than his, but Babur's had matchlocks and two cannon, plus the advice of two specialists in Ottoman tactics. The cannon were especially effective against the enemy's elephants, who were as unprepared for firearms as mammoths had been for atlatls. The next year at Kanua the Mughals again were inferior in numbers. They countered the charge of 80,000 cavalry and 500 elephants with gunpowder weapons and won again.

The greatest of the Mughal emperors was Babur's grandson, Akbar, a gunpowder enthusiast who inspected every new cannon personally. In 1568 he won the city of Chitor with the aid of three large batteries of artillery dragged to the site and a giant cannon cast on the spot. The next year he invested the fortress at Ranthambor, battering its walls with fifteen siege cannon dragged into place by hundreds of bullocks and elephants. It surrendered in a month.[17]

Far away, in the northern nimbus of the Hearthland, a third great gunpowder empire arose. Ivan III, Grand Prince of Muscovy, utilized imported guns to break loose from Mongol domination and to humble rivals, and at the end of the fifteenth century proclaimed himself as ruler of all Russia. The next Ivan, the fourth, known as the Terrible (meaning awesome rather the horrendous, though he was that too), inherited his predecessor's imperial ambitions and penchant for firearms. When the younger Ivan led his

---

[17] John F. Richards, *The New Cambridge History of India*, Part I. Vol. 5, *The Mughal Empire*, (Cambridge: Cambridge University Press, 1987), 6–8, 10, 26–7; Halil Inalcik, "The Socio-political Effects of the Diffusion of Firearms in the Middle East" in *War, Technology and Society in the Middle East*, eds. V. J. Parry and M. E. Yapp (London: Oxford University Press, 1975), 204; Needham, *Science and Civilisation in China*, 5, Part 7, 442; Zaman, *Mughal Artillery*, 6, 7, 17, 40.

armies east and southeast against those heirlooms from the Mongol imperium, the Khanates of Kazan and of Astrakhan, where firearms were rare and tactics to counter them unfamiliar, he did well. Where he could bring his companies of harquebuses and, most particularly, his bombards with him, via barge and sleigh, he did well, indeed. In 1552 he broke the wooden walls of Kazan with 150 artillery pieces. (And a giant trebuchet as well. New equipment was fine, but no reason to forgo use of the old.) When he was done, his empire included the entire valley of the Volga to the Caspian Sea.

Before Ivan the Terrible died, Ermak Timofeevich, a Cossack, led a force armed with gunpowder weapons across the Urals into Siberia and so began the expansion of the Czarist empire to the Pacific.[18]

Gunpowder fueled the rise of new centers of power wherever in Eurasia and Africa aggressive leaders waived military tradition and "jumped the gun" in adopting the new weapons. But many factors other than gunpowder, for and against and at cross purposes, operated there, and the picture is far from crystal clear. It is in the isolation of the islands of the Pacific that we can observe the nearly unadulterated political effect of gunpowder. Gunpowder entered the lives of the islanders in, relatively speaking, an instant, and their remoteness from mainland populations saved them from immediate subjugation or the fear thereof. The Hawaiians, the people of the most remote of the planet's major inhabitable archipelagos, who passed centuries in nearly hermetic isolation until 1778, supply an especially uncomplicated example.

They coveted all the wonderful things Captain Cook and his men had brought with them on the *Resolution* and the *Discovery* from over the horizon in that year. Among the more fascinating

---

[18] McNeill, *Age of Gunpowder Empires,* 27–8; Janet Martin, *Medieval Russia, 980–1584* (Cambridge: Cambridge University Press, 1996), 351–4, 357–9.

were muskets and cannon, which the interlopers used to frighten off the Hawaiians, and then, when the novelty wore thin, to wound and kill to demonstrate that there was more to these devices than flash and bang.

The culmination of such gross attempts at communication occurred on the expedition's second visit to the islands in 1779, when Cook fired one barrel of his musket to warn, the second to kill, and was killed himself immediately afterward. The members of his shore party either died on the spot or fled, leaving their firearms behind, the first to pass into Hawaiian possession.[19]

In the next decade more Europeans and Americans as well paused in Hawaii for victuals, water and, often, sex. In exchange, the Hawaiians insisted on metal articles, clothing, hats and so on and gunpowder weaponry.[20] If they pressed hard, which they often did, they sometimes got more of the latter than they wanted, as in 1790 when the American merchantman, the *Eleanor,* delivered a broadside, which killed more than a hundred of them. Soon after the Hawaiians seized another ship, the *Fair American,* with firearms and a surviving *haole* (white) to fire them.

Kamehameha, a chief whom one visitor called "as sordid as a white man," took possession of those prizes and, in the coming years, acquired more arms and powder and additional *haole* aides. (He and his rivals would have been as happy to have Turkish gunners as any Mughal prince, but none were available.) By 1804 he had six hundred muskets, fourteen cannon, forty swivels, and six small mortars.[21]

[19] Gavan Daws, *Shoals of Time: A History of the Hawaiian Islands* (Honolulu: University of Hawaii Press, 1968), 1–32; Ralph S. Kuykendall, *The Hawaiian Kingdom* (Honlulu: University Press of Hawaii, 1968), Vol. 1, 19.

[20] Patrick V. Kirch and Marshall Sahlins, *Anahulu: The Anthropology of History in the Kingdom of Hawaii* (Chicago: University of Chicago Press, 1992), 37–43.

[21] Kirch and Sahlins, *Anahulu,* 43.

In the years around the turn of the nineteenth century, hundreds, perhaps thousands, of Hawaiians died to advance or stymie Kamehameha's effort to do what had never been done before: unify the islands. One of the battles, a characteristic one, was called *Kepuwahaulaula*, the battle of the red-mouthed gun. Kamehameha's army won the climatic battle, fought in 1795 in the smoke of guns in the Nuuanu valley above what would become the city of Honolulu.[22] Kamehameha was the last of the classic gunpowder emperors.

On the other side of the world and to the west of the gunpowder empires of the sultans and czars, the political situation when gunpowder weaponry arrived was similar to that in Japan when the Portuguese showed up with harquebuses. Western Europe also had an imperial tradition, that of Rome, but was in fact a decentralized hodgepodge of political units – city-states, dukedoms, baronies, bishoprics, and what-have-you – some of which were always at war. "Italy" and "Germany" were words of geographical but no precise political definition. There were kingdoms in Europe – as, for instance, the kings of France and England certainly claimed – but they fell far short of being centralized nation-states. There were kings and perhaps popes too, who dreamed of reigning over a Eurowide gunpowder empire, but none of them succeeded.

Europe took gunpowder to its bosom like a lover's bouquet. On February 11, 1326, the Council of Florence appointed two officers to make bullets and cannon for the defense of the republic, which is early indeed in the history of actual firearms.[23] In that century the

<hr />

[22] Kuykendall, *Hawaiian Kingdom*, Vol. 1, 47; K. R. Howe, *Where the Waves Fall: A New South Islands History from First Settlement to Colonial Rule* (Honolulu: University of Hawaii Press, 1984), 155–7.

[23] Needham, *Science and Civilisation in China*, Vol. 5, Pt. 7, 284–341; Partington, *A History of Greek Fire and Gunpowder*, 101; Hogg, *Artillery: Its Origin, Heyday and Decline*, 32, 34; Cipolla, *Guns, Sails, and Empires*, opposite 96.

West's firearms may have been inferior to China's, but the latter's would improve slowly and the former's relatively swiftly. In the following century the Ottoman Empire would seem to have had most of the biggest bombards, but often the Turks, as in the case of Urban, Mehmed II's favorite gun-founder, drew their gunpowder gurus from the Balkans, Italy, and elsewhere in Europe.

Europe's natural advantage was good deposits of metal ores, and its natural disadvantage, stemming from its temperate climate, was meager deposits of saltpeter. For a long while the Europeans had to make their own. One of their first saltpeter "plantations" shows up in the record in Frankfurt in 1388. The recipe for making saltpeter was simple: dump barnyard accumulations in a pit or vat, marinate in urine for a year, dig up, strain, wash, boil, and you have your saltpeter.[24] Making saltpeter was a lot of trouble, but the West's ambitious kings needed a lot of it.

The most stubborn obstacles in their way were walls. At first the kings had no projectile weapon for breaching those walls better than the trebuchet, which was some help but not enough. How, for instance, was the French king to win the Hundred Years War and unify his country if the English backpedaled not across the Channel but into their castles in Normandy to sit and wait until the French army wore down and went away (Fig. 11).

Bombards like Mons Meg, at present on exhibit at Edinburgh Castle, were the answer to the French king's problem. This fifteenth-century monster is thirteen feet long, nineteen inches in caliber, and weighs five tons. It fired a ball (of stone, as was usual with early bombards, rather than of iron) that weighed 330 pounds.[25]

---

[24] Gerhard W. Kramer, "*Das Feuerwerkbuch;* Its Importance in the Early History of Black Powder" in *Gunpowder: The History of an International Technology,* ed. Brenda J. Buchanan (Bath: Bath University Press, 1996), 51.

[25] Geoffrey Parker, *The Military Revolution: Military Innovation and the Rise of the West, 1500–1800* (Cambridge: Cambridge University Press, 1996), 7.

Figure 11. European field artillery of the mid-fifteenth century. Also, note fire bombs being launched by crossbows. *German Firework Book*, c. 1450.

The French spiritual hero of the war was the saintly Joan of Arc, but the English burned her in 1431 and continued in occupation of much of France. The French hero of the last years of the war was (or should have been) the technologically adept Maître Jean Bureau, a ghost from the future described as "of humble origins and small stature, but a man of purpose and daring." He, another of the mobile technicians, probably started as a gunner for the English and then switched sides. His guns and others served the French king well, for a while knocking off castles in Normandy at a rate of five a month. He was the key figure in the siege of Bordeaux, the last city held by the English in France. It surrendered on October 19, 1453, and soon after the king appointed Bureau, despite his common origins, its mayor for life.[26]

Gunpowder figured in the formation of such nation-states as England, France, and Spain, but soon the momentum for a further centralization faltered. The gunpowder genie had gotten loose in the West and spread to many polities. The new projectile technology didn't climax with the bombards and a single authority's triumph in Europe.

The French and Burgundians discovered that smaller but stronger cannon firing dense iron cannonballs with better gunpowder could wreak as much or more damage as the old-fashioned bombards with their stone balls. The French further realized that a cannon's mobility was as important as its muzzle velocity, and put their new ordnance on full gun carriages. In the 1490s they rolled into Italy, battering and plundering all the way to Naples. Machiavelli despaired: "No wall exists, however thick, that

---

[26] Needham, *Science and Civilisation in China*, Vol. 5, Pt. 7, 16.; Desmond Seward, *The Hundred Years War: The English in France, 1337–1453* (New York: Antheum, 1978), 247, 249, 252, 257–9, 262.

artillery cannot destroy in a few days."[27] Perhaps the emperor of Western Europe would be French.

That was not to be: the French were only a bit quicker at utilizing gunpowder weaponry than rivals, who were soon acquiring the improved cannons and setting them on carriages too. There was also a renaissance in the techniques of fortification, a depressing portent for centripetalists because they *had* to be able to knock down walls.

The French invaders taught the Italians that vertical masonry walls could not resist cannon fire. In desperation, they threw up thick sloping ridges of heaped soil, and, lo, discovered that these absorbed cannon balls and survived to block the attackers. The ditch in front of the rampart from which the dirt had been dug served as a obstacle to the attacking forces too. How do you blast away a ditch?

This style of fortification, *trace italienne,* with stone facings and jutting bastions to afford defenders flanking fire, became standard throughout much of the West. (Cannon inspired a counterpart style in east Asia too, one of massive walls, multiple moats, and intricate design, but seemingly not of such abrupt and decisive influence as in the West.)[28] The *trace italienne* designers, like gunfounders, found themselves in a lucrative international business. Leonardo da Vinci tried his hand at it, as did Michelangelo, who once advertised himself as not knowing "much about painting and sculpture, but I have gained great experience of fortification."[29]

[27] McNeill, *Age of Gunpowder Empires,* 6, 7; William H. McNeill, *The Pursuit of Power: Technology, Armed Force, and Society since A.D. 1,000* (Chicago: University of Chicago Press, 1984), 88; Cipolla, *Guns, Sails, and Empires,* 27–8; Geoffrrey Paarker, *The Military Revolution: Military Innovation and the Rise of the West,* 2nd ed. (Cambridge: Cambridge University Press, 1999), 164.

[28] Delmer M. Brown, "The Impact of Firearms on Japanese Warfare, 1543–98" in *Technology and European Overseas Enterprise,* 95–6, 101.

[29] Parker, *The Military Revolution: Military Innovation and the Rise of the West, 1500–1800,* 10–12; John Keegan, *A History of Warfare* (New York: Alfred A. Knopf, 1993), 325.

The West's frog-march to centralization slowed and halted far short of a Eurowide empire. The effect of gunpowder weaponry was to encourage and maintain a wobbly but amazingly durable assemblage of competing entities.[30]

At some moment in the sixteenth century the forces driving the creation of gunpowder empires of contiguous land holdings within the Hearthland faltered. No great power, most particularly not in the West, held a monopoly of the new weaponry, and methods to counter or defend against it were spreading. The Europeans, probably because they were almost constantly at war with each other, were the most energetic and inventive of those who made and used gunpowder. Frustrated in their wars to build contiguous empires at home, they supplemented these with efforts to create discontiguous empires overseas.

An unvoidable obstacle to building any overseas empires in the first millennia of recorded history had been that watercraft accommodated only minor and close-range weaponry and most of the men on board were not soldiers or prospective colonists but rowers and indispensable as such. By 1400 the peoples of the Hearthland were closing in on solutions to these problems. The Ming Chinese assembled fleets including the largest vessels anywhere and sent them as far as the coasts of east Africa. Then China's elites lost interest in external contacts and persuaded the Emperor to forbid such adventuring and even trading overseas, anticipating the Japanese in this policy by some three hundred years. The world's first overseas empire was not to be Chinese.

By the end of the fifteenth century western Europeans of the Atlantic coasts had vessels, lateen and square-rigged, that, though small by Chinese standards, were suitable for oceanic crossings. They relied on sail and so their crew and passengers were available for tasks other than rowing. These vessels carried cannon, at first

---

[30] McNeill, *Pursuit of Power,* 90–1.

only at bow and stern, and then along the gunwales, no longer monopolized by rowers and oars. In the beginning these cannon were topside, few in number and of small caliber because too much weight on the top deck destabilized the vessels. In the sixteenth century, Europeans began to launch ships broader at the lower deck or decks than the top deck, so that large cannon could be mounted below, stabilizing the ship with weight near the waterline, and firing through gun ports. An English Commission of Reform summed it up, succinctly if tardily, in 1618:

> Experience teacheth how sea-fights in these days come seldome to boarding or to great execution of bow, arrow, small shot and the swords, but are chiefly performed by the great artillery breaking down masts, yards, tearing, raking and bilging the ships, wherein the great advantage of His Majesty's navy must carefully be maintained by appointing such a proportion of ordnance to each ship as the vessel will bear.[31]

Now the biggest of the new artillery, the successors of the bombards, could be swiftly shipped (literally) into the ports and off the coasts of an enemy or prospective thrall and do what bombards had been doing to castles for generations. And the ships could carry human cargoes of fighters and colonists.[32] The West's nearest equivalents of the Middle East's gunpowder empires would be overseas empires.

Gunpowder was a protagonist in the drama of European imperialism everywhere, but did not guarantee victory everywhere. Firearms were old among the peoples of littoral Asia when the Europeans appeared on their coasts and the defenders, who knew or soon learned how to shoot back, delayed the high tide of white imperialism until the invaders returned with improved ordnance in

---

[31] Cipolla, *Guns, Sails and Empires*, 86.
[32] Cipolla, *Guns, Sails and Empires*, 81–2.

the nineteenth century. Such was also the case in sub-Saharan Africa, with a somewhat different twist. Firearms arrived as early as the 1400s, but the Africans did not adopt the new weapons in quantities for another two or three centuries, when their importation soared with the increase in violence associated with the slave trade. As one Dutch factor put it in a startling metaphor, we traders are "obliging them with a knife to cut their own throats."[33] Even so, disease, climate, and resilient resistance made the prize of territorial conquest not worth the price until the rifle replaced the musket and the advent of the Maxim gun in, again, the nineteenth century.

It was in the New World (and Siberia, too, as already mentioned), where the Europeans triumph was nearly total. There the locals had no knowledge or even warning of gunpowder. Montaigne remarked on the effects in America of "the lightning flashes of our cannons, the thundering of our harquebuses (able to confuse the mind of Caesar himself in his day if they had surprised him when he was as ignorant of them as they were)."[34]

Soon after arriving on the coast of Cuba in 1492, Columbus made a show of his weapons to the inhabitants, the Tainos. He had one of his company shoot a "Turkish bow" (no doubt a composite bow) and then, the piece de résistance, had a cannon and a musket fired. The locals fell to the earth, and then honored Columbus with a gift of a golden mask.[35]

---

[33] R. A. Kea, "Firearms and Warfare on the Gold and Slave Coasts from the Sixteenth to the Nineteenth Centuries" in *Technology and European Overseas Enterprise*, 116; J. E. Inikori, "The Import of Firearms into West Africa, 1750–1807" in *Warfare and Empires: Contact and Conflict between European and Non-European Military and Maritime Forces and Cultures*, ed. Douglas M. Peers (Ashgate, Aldershot, UK: Variorum, 1997), 245–74.

[34] Michel de Montaigne, *The Complete Essays*, trans. M. A. Screech (London: Penguin Books, 1987), 1030.

[35] *Journals and Other Documents on the Life and Voyages of Christopher Columbus*, trans. and ed., Samuel Eliot Morison (New York: Heritage Press, 1963), 137–8.

Hernán Cortés resorted to the same theatrics in Mexico. He ordered a cannon fired for the edification of the first emissaries from the Aztec empire, who "fell to the floor as if dead." They reported the thunder to Moctezuma and that something like a ball had come out from inside the cannon and had "turned a tree to dust; it seemed to make it vanish, as though someone had conjured it away."[36]

The propaganda effect of gunpowder's flash and thunder soon faded, but by then the Europeans had their foothold, after which gunpowder's effectiveness as a killer came into play. Cannon were, for example, particularly useful during the Spanish siege of Tenochtitlán (Mexico City) for clearing the causeways and then the streets of the Aztec soldiers.[37]

America's indigenes were as impressed by firearms on first acquaintance as the Mongols, Persians, Italians, et al. had been and like these soon adopted the new weapons. For example, in New England the indigenes accounted "their bows and arrows but baubles in comparison with them" and "would not stick to give any price they could attain for them." But these naifs and equivalents elsewhere in the Americas took up firearms to less advantage than had the peoples of the Hearthland. The latter, even the laggards, usually were technologically advanced enough to acquire not only the new weapons but the techniques by which to produce them.[38] The naifs, on the other hand, who knew nothing whatsoever of gunpowder, nothing of iron and steel, and, the most

---

[36] *We People Here: Nahuatl Accounts of the Conquest of Mexico*, ed and trans. James Lockhart (Berkeley: University of California Press, 1993), 80–1.

[37] Bernal Díaz del Castillo, *The Discovery and Conquest of Mexico*, trans. A. P. Maudslay (New York: Farrar, Straus and Giroux, 1959), 404, 407.

[38] Sub-Saharan Africans were slow to do so also, though they had an old and strong tradition of iron smithing. This suggests that there is more to adopting a technology than reflex action. See John K. Thornton, *Warfare in Atlantic Africa* (London: UCL Press, 1999), 151.

remote of them, nothing even of the bow and arrow, acquired guns but not gunsmiths. They often became highly skilled in repairing firearms (as did the Africans) and even molded their own shot, but could not produce even their own guns or gunpowder. They became dependent on their enemies, the invaders.[39]

By 1800 Europeans occupied or controlled 35 percent of the land surface of the globe.[40]

[39] Patrick M. Malone, "Changing Military Technology among the Indians of Southern New England, 1600–1677" in *Warfare and Empires*, 232m 237–8.

[40] Daniel R. Headrick, *The Tools of Empire: Technology and European Imperialism in the Nineteenth Century* (New York: Oxford University Press, 1981), 3.

EIGHT

Brown Bess to Big Bertha

I do maintain and will prove whenever called upon that no man was ever killed at 200 yards by a common musket by the person who aimed at him.

Colonel Hanger (1814)[1]

What passing-bells for these who die as cattle?
  Only the monstrous anger of the guns.
  Only the stuttering rifles' rapid rattle.
Can patter out their hasty orisons.

  Wilfrid Owen, "Anthem for Doomed Youth" (1918)

While the world in the middle centuries of the second millenium C.E. worked out the military and geopolitical consequences of the Chinese invention of gunpowder, projectile technology per se lagged and stagnated. The obvious applications of igniting gunpowder in tubes to expel missiles or to drive tubes through the air

---

[1] B. P. Hughes, *Firepower: Weapons Effectiveness on the Battlefield, 1630–1850* (New York: Sarpedon, 1997), 26.

as missiles were accomplished, at least crudely, long before 1500. From then to the nineteenth century, gunsmiths, gun-founders, and rocket makers produced many thousands – millions, more likely – of these devices, but accomplished nothing to compare with the Song Dynasty breakthrough. They produced stronger cannons and gunpowder in kernels rather than a powder ("corned" gunpowder), which burned better. They put cannons on carriages and then on better carriages, invented explosive shells and stuffed them with grape shot, fastened long trailing sticks to rockets to improve their accuracy, and so on, but all that was no more than bringing European changes on the old Chinese themes.

Ian V. Hogg, noted historian of artillery, suggests that if one of King Edward III's gunners at Crécy in 1346 had been transferred to 1870 and service in the Franco-Prussian War, he would soon have felt at home: "In the five hundred or so years since the invention of the cannon there had been little technical advance."[2] Quibblers might want to snip a century's worth of years off the ends of that half millennium to ensure the accuracy of the appraisal – cannon in 1346 were still very primitive and rifled breech-loaders had at least arrived by 1870– but the statement is sound.

Most big cannon in the late Renaissance and practically all of every size in 1800 were muzzle-loaders, the charging of which was slow and laborious and accomplished by the gunners getting out in front and exposing themselves to enemy missiles. The cannon had smooth bores, fired cannon*balls*, and were, therefore, short-ranged; their missiles emerged from the muzzles spinning wildly and veering unpredictably.[3]

In 1800, as in 1500, handguns and shoulder firearms, the standard infantry weapons, were similarly deficient. Matchlocks, flint-

---

[2] Ian V. Hogg, *The Guns, 1914–18* (New York: Ballantine Books, 1971), 9–10. See also Bert S. Hall, *Weapons and Warfare in Renaissance Europe* (Baltimore: Johns Hopkins University Press, 1997), 156.

[3] Hughes, *Firepower,* 29–35.

locks, and muskets were loaded by standing up to manipulate a ramrod, with the soldier defenseless and exposed. Not even the most adept could load, aim, and fire more than a few times a minute. The smooth bore barrels delivered a spherical missile, and were wildly inaccurate at ranges of over a hundred meters.[4]

No wonder that in 1814 a Colonel Hanger sputtered that if you fired at a man at two hundred yards with a common musket, you had no better chance of hitting your target than if you had fired at the moon.[5] His muskets were less apt to misfire than sixteenth-century matchlocks, but they weren't more accurate.

The saga of the Brown Bess serves nicely as a synecdoche for gunpowder technology in the mid-centuries of its history. That musket, so inaccurate that it wasn't even fitted with sights, was the British infantry's standard arm from 1690 to 1840, a period of 150 years. That is as many years as passed between the Millimete arrow-firing cannon and Mehemed II's wall-shattering bombards, or between Bess's retirement and the V-2 rocket.[6]

The saga of rockets from the time of their first development through the nineteenth century isn't as neat as Bess's tale, but is instructive and – a lagniappe – at the end cheering, a rare phenomenon in the history of projectile technology.

The rocket became a staple in Hearthland warfare about the same time as guns for good reasons. Rocketeers required less training than cannoneers; their weapon's range was similar to the cannon's and was cheaper and much more portable. A man could walk with a standard rocket on his shoulder to wherever it was needed. William Congreve, of whom we will have more in a few pages, described rockets as "the soul of artillery without its encumbrance."

---

[4] Hughes, *Firepower*, 10, 26; Hugh B. Pollard, *Pollard's History of Firearms*, ed. Claude Blair (New York: Macmillan, 1983), 29–31, 42, 55, 62, 67.

[5] Hughes, *Firepower*, 26.

[6] William H. McNeill, *The Pursuit of Power: Technology, Armed Force, and Society since A.D. 1000* (Chicago: University of Chicago Press, 1982), 142.

And, of course, there was no problem of recoil with rockets. Light the fuse, get out of the way, both front and back (compulsory), and off the missile went.

Rockets had disadvantages too, of course. Stuffing them with gunpowder could lead to premature explosions, and the powder, which might reside in the rocket casing for a long time, would sometimes ignite spontaneously or, alternatively, absorb so much moisture that it wouldn't ignite at all. Worst of all was the rocket's inaccuracy. It might whiz right at the enemy, but probably not, and it might hook or slice or sometimes even turn round and come back. Rockets, however, were useful when fired in large numbers at big targets and were good for panicking green troops and horses.

The Mughals, whose interest in firearms sagged after Akbar's triumphs, favored rockets.[7] François Bernier, in 1658 an eyewitness to the battle at Samugarh between Mughal brothers, describes the *ban*, a rocket, usually of iron, a dozen or so centimeters long, loaded with gunpowder and fixed to a stick or arrow. The rocketeer would light its fuse and, in most cases, throw it overhand like a javelin (getting rid of it immediately was important). Then, while it was in the air, its gunpowder propellant would ignite and carry the arrow as far as a thousand meters or more.[8] It might strike and disable a soldier or horse or, if it carried incendiary material, ignite and destroy something important, but its value was chiefly psychological. Captain Thomas Williamson, another observer, wrote that, "all fly from the hissing winding visitor, receiving perhaps a smart stroke from the stick, which gives direction to the tube and often causes it to make the most sudden and unexpected traverses."[9]

7 Frank H. Winter, *The First Golden Age of Rocketry: Congreve and Hale Rockets of the Nineteenth Century* (Washington, DC: Smithsonian Institution Press, 1990), 47–9, 77–9; John F. Richards, *The Mughal Empire* (Cambridge: Cambridge University Press, 1998), 142–3, 288–9.

8 Needham, *Science and Civilisation in China*, Vol. 5, Part 7, *Military Technology; The Gunpowder Epic* (Cambridge: Cambridge University Press), 517.

9 M. K. Zaman, *Mughal Artillery* (Delhi: Vishal Printers, 1983), 14–15.

Wars fought in the aftermath of the Mughal Empire in the eighteenth century between the English East India Company and Mysore rekindled European interest in rockets. Among the interested was William Congreve, who, in a portent of things to come, had written at the age of thirteen that he was "fully bent on going to the Moon." (His proposed vehicle – he hadn't seen or heard of India's rockets yet – was the balloon.)[10]

Congreve's first rockets were inferior to India's, but he was confident, meticulous, and patient – a man of the Industrial Revolution. He improved the gunpowder that drove his rockets, packaged them in strong iron casings, provided longer and stronger guide-sticks, eventually moving these from the side to the center of the rocket's axis, improving accuracy, and he worked out the angle at which the rocket should be launched for maximum range. By the summer of 1805 he had a number of varieties, standardized and tipped with dependable incendiary warheads. In 1807 the British used his rockets in the attack on Copenhagen, a good broad target, burning down much of the city.[11]

Congreve's rockets figured in several battles in the next years. For Americans the most important of these (though not one that they expend much effort to commemorate) took place in August 1813 at Bladensburg near Washington, D.C. American militia made a respectable showing against invading British forces until subjected to a barrage of British rockets. These green troops had never faced such hissing, whizzing intimidation before. Like, no doubt, similarly inexperienced soldiers of China's enemies centuries earlier, like the Ashanti at Akantamasu, Ghana, a few years later, they

---

[10] Winter, *The First Golden Age of Rocketry*, 13. Winter's is the best book on nineteenth-century rocketry, but a useful summary can be found in H. C. B. Rogers, *A History of Artillery* (Secaucus, NJ: Citadel Press, 1975), 95–209.

[11] Winter, *First Golden Age of Rocketry*, 15, 19, 20–2.

panicked and ran.[12] On the night of August 24, 1813, the British burned the U.S. capitol.

The British fleet, which included Congreve's rocket ship, the appropriately named *Erebus*, sailed up the Chesapeake to torch Baltimore, but couldn't get past Fort McHenry. Francis Scott Key, an American, watched and then wrote, "And the rockets' red glare, the bombs bursting in air, gave proof thro' the night that our flag was still there." His poem became his nation's national anthem. The flag in question, with holes, some of them probably made by Congreve's rockets, is usually on public display at the Smithsonian Institution a few minutes' walk from the capitol building that replaced the one the British burned.[13]

Congreve indulged in Peenemündean visions of rockets of a ton in weight with warheads powerful enough to breach the walls of any fortress, but attracted little support. Rockets were employed in the major and many minor wars of the next fifty years, most prominently in the Crimean War, but rarely with much success as compared to firearms. In 1856, in the Second Opium War, the Chinese launched their own rockets against British ships in the Canton River, with the kinds of results often cited by rocketry's detractors. One rocket did burn a hole in a British ship, but Admiral Kennedy wrote that "as a rule the Chinese rockets did little harm, as often as not doubling back from whence they came."[14]

Technicians and inventors continued to work on rockets, increasing their size (somewhat), range (a lot), and even their accuracy. William Hale made a rocket with canted exhaust holes instead of the long, awkward, and ineffective stick, spinning the missile for

---

[12] Winter, *First Golden Age of Rocketry*, 41; Needham, *Science and Civilisation in China*, Vol. 5, Pt. 7, 474–5.

[13] Winter, *First Golden Age of Rocketry*, 24–6.

[14] Winter, *First Golden Age of Rocketry*, 41, 52; Needham, *Science and Civilisation in China*, Vol. 5, Part 7, 520.

stability in flight and greatly improving its accuracy. But, as the decades passed, rockets figured in fewer and fewer conflicts and only rarely in any decisive way, except in a few battles on the frontiers of Europe's overseas empires where the indigenes, like the Americans at Bladensberg, had never been subjected to such fire before.

History is often ironic, as was the case with nineteenth-century rocketry, but rarely so sweetly so. The Hale rocket became an essential tool not for governmental institutions of violence, armies and navies, but for their lifesaving services. Sailors and passengers in vessels foundering in waters too rough for rescue boats could now, for the first time, be helped. Rockets carrying block, tackle, and trailing lines could be fired via Hale rocket over the vessels. The beleaguered sailors could fix these to their masts and could ride by breeches buoy over the waves to safety. In the 1870s a total of 9,407 were so rescued on England's lifesaving service alone.[15]

It seems odd, at a glance, that progress in rocketry was so slight in the nineteenth century when the Hearthland, this time not at its eastern but the other end, was entering another of its deliriums of invention. The West made advances in projectile technology in firearms that were so impressive as to relegate rockets to the back shelf.

These improvements were one part of what historians call the Industrial Revolution, and should be considered along with its other parts. Steam locomotives and ships made possible the transportation to the battlefield of ordnance of enormous size and weight and of ammunition in unprecedented quantities. New steels, tools to minutely shape materials, and mass production of interchangeable parts, revolutionized the design, production, and use of weaponry. In the second half of the century rapid-fire breech-loaders, both small arms and cannon, with rifled barrels and per-

15 Winter, *First Golden Age of Rocketry*, 231, 235.

cussion caps instead of smoldering matches or flints, began to replace the old weapons.[16]

These changed the nature of battle. Clear evidence of this came with the Crimean War and the American Civil War, in which weapons with rifled barrels were employed with devastating effect, obliging soldiers to take refuge in trenches and dugouts. The lesson, not absorbed for more than a half century, was that simpleminded, frontal assaults by foot soldiers were now out-of-date.

The American war inspired the invention of the first machine gun that actually worked, at least in demonstrations, the multibarreled, crank-operated Gatling gun. Richard Gatling boasted that his weapon was to muskets as the McCormack reaper was to the sickle or the sewing machine to the common needle. He thought that it would

> by its rapidity of fire enable one man to do as much battle duty as a hundred, that it would to a great extent, supersede the necessity of large armies, and consequently exposure to battle and disease would be greatly diminished.[17]

His prediction proved valid only for wars between societies that had the new weapon and those that did not. The Anglo-French poet Hillaire Belloc wrote of the most renowned of the single-barreled, fully automatic successors to the Gatling gun, "Thank God that we have got/The Maxim gun, and they have not."[18]

In the same middle decades of the century, others like Gatling and Maxim turned out the first practical breech-loading cannons with rifled barrels and fitted them with hydraulic buffers to tame their recoil. These fired, for greater accuracy and penetration, not

[16] Rogers, *A History of Artillery*, 93.
[17] John Ellis, *The Social History of the Machine Gun* (Baltimore: Johns Hopkins University Press, 1986), 16, 27.
[18] Ellis, *Social History of the Machine Gun*, 18.

cannon balls but elongated shells. By the end of the century, quick-firing field artillery with rifled barrels – the French 75 is the classic example – were essential components in the armies of every major power.[19]

The new advances in gun-founding produced worthy successors to Mehemed's ponderous bombards. Steam locomotives could get the biggest ones to strategic locations in the territories of the advanced nations. Steam-driven warships, which had no need of masts and complicated rigging, became conveyances for huge cannon. These ironclads could sidle up to every important coast and far up the rivers and freely distribute death and destruction wherever they went.

The new guns, land and sea, small arms and cannon, were longer ranged than those of the past and much more destructive because the age of black powder was over. Guncotton, cordite, and other new and more powerful explosives drove shells and bullets harder and farther, and shells loaded with them exploded more destructively on arrival.

In the last decades of the nineteenth century the new cannon and rifles gave a greater advantage to Europe over the rest of the world, excepting such offspring as the United States, than any comparable region had ever had before.[20] That advantage was comparable to that which the Cro-Magnons with their atlatls had over the Neanderthals, presuming (a prodigious assumption) that the former possessed the projectile launcher and the latter did not.

During the peak years of the West's projectile superiority, its victims, in their desperation, sometimes resorted to magic. Boxer rebels in China convinced themselves that rituals would protect

[19] Winter, *First Golden Age of Rocketry*, 193, 212, 213; Rogers, *History of Artillery*, 128.

[20] Daniel R. Headrick, *The Tools of Empire: Technology and European Imperialism in the Nineteenth Century* (New York: Oxford University Press, 1981), 6–7.

them from the Westerners' missiles. In New Zealand the Hauhau chanted certain words and in the U.S. Amerindian followers of the Ghost Dance religion donned special shirts for the same purpose and with the same result.

Joseph Conrad, who as a young man worked in the Congo, witnessed Europeans in full exercise of their superiority and was impressed with its superficiality. He wrote of a French man-o-war shelling at some target inland: "Pop, would go one of the six-inch guns; a small flame would dart and vanish, a little white smoke would disappear, a tiny projectile would give a feeble screech – and nothing happened."[21] True enough, perhaps, for that day or that month, but in terms of years a lot did happen. In 1800 the West had controlled 35 percent of the land surface of the world. In 1914 it controlled 84 percent.[22] That state of affairs, as Conrad, if asked, might have predicted, proved short-lived, but its effect was permanent and titanic.

The new projectile technology drove vast changes within the West as well. The new weapons did not, any more than smooth-bore weapons had, settle the rivalries of the nation-states that had emerged in the early centuries of the gunpowder era, but they did make their collisions appallingly more destructive and bloodier. World War I began in August 1914 with a general expectation that it would shortly end with victory by *our* (define this word as you will) side. The Central Powers, chief among them Germany, had the great advantage of being just that, central. They could react quickly and shift forces from front to front along short lines of internal transport. Their and Germany's great disadvantage was also centrality: they were surrounded.

[21] Joseph Conrad, *Heart of Darkness* (Norwalk, CT: Easton Press, 1980), 19.
[22] Headrick, *The Tools of Empire*, 3.

Germany could not draw on the resources of the world and was unlikely to win a long war. It would have to move much faster than its opponents, the Allies. It would have to have and use new and devastating weapons. It might have to wage war on the Allies' civilians.

Germany's first strategy for coping with a two-front war was the Schlieffin Plan: rapid advance through Belgium to destroy and neutralize the armies defending France, and then a quick turnabout eastward to join the Austrians in a leisurely destruction of Russia's forces. The major obstacle in the path of the forces ordered to plunge through Belgium into France in August 1918 was the fortress complex around Liège, the end product of a half millennium of countering advances in artillery with thicker walls, deeper ditches, and more and bigger guns, now in armor-plated turrets like those of battleships. An army that conquered them could do so by siege, which would make a farce of Schlieffin's schedule, or would have to quickly bash them into rubble, which would require bombards to dwarf Mehemed's.

Germany's bombard was a 42-centimeter howitzer.[23] This behemoth was a product of the House of Krupp and its steel founders and cannon makers. The howitzer was called *die dicke Bertha,* Big Bertha, in honor of the matriarch of the Krupp family, Bertha Krupp von Bohlen (an honor she accepted "with resignation"). A forty-ton cannon, it fired an 1,800-pound (820-kilogram) shell in an arc nearly 5 kilometers high and 14 kilometers in length. On August 12, 1918, the first of these fell on Belgian territory. The sound of its explosion was so loud that Belgians thought an entire fort's magazine had exploded.

The German gunners found the range on Fort Pontisse with their eighth shell, which dropped right on and through the fort's concrete roof. They fired more shells, the fort surrendered at 12:30

---

[23] Barbara W. Tuckman, *The Guns of August* (New York: Macmillan, 1962), 166–7.

the next day, and the Big Berthas proceeded on to Liège's other forts. All of these forts, designed, manned, and supplied to survive for months, surrendered in four days. The Big Berthas had done as well as Mehemed's bombards, only much faster.[24]

The German forces moved forward more swiftly than the Allies had believed possible, but not swiftly enough to win the war. The French and British stitched together an adequate defense and the Western Front became a killing field in which for four years an advance or retreat of a thousand meters was considered significant. The new ordnance like the nimble French 75, the Big Bertha, and Allied equivalents, supposed to blow a path through enemy lines, instead churned the land into a porridge through which rapid advance was very difficult. The machine gun mowed down attackers like, to recall Gatling's remark, a McCormack reaper mowing grain, rendering traditional exercise of courage stupid. "A long burst of machine gun does not kill a battalion," wrote one witness,

> some men in a line will almost certainly pass through the run of bullets, in the gaps between them, so to speak. But if the line of men perseveres with a determined gallantry, over an open approach, the end is certain.[25]

The casualty rates on the Western Front where the German fought the French, British Empire, and American armies soared to levels undreamed of in 1914. There were 3,600 soldiers in Adolph Hitler's regiment, the 16th Bavarian Reserve, when it took up position in the line; only 611 were alive and unwounded a month later.[26] A British officer and poet, Robert Graves, on the other side

[24] Hogg, *The Guns, 1914–18*, 33–43; William Manchester, *The Arms of Krupp* (New York: Bantam Books, 1970), 3, 278.
[25] Ellis, *Social History of the Machine Gun*, 136.
[26] John Keegan, *A History of Warfare* (New York: Alfred A. Knopf, 1933), 359.

of No Man's Land, recalled with a snarl later what the experience
had been like:

> And we recall the merry ways of guns –
> Nibbling the walls of factory and church
> Like as child, piecrust, felling groves of trees
> Like a child, dandelions with a switch!
> Machine-guns rattle toy-like from a hill,
> Down in a row the brave tin-soldiers fall...[27]

The soldiers on both sides went to ground like moles and dug
trench lines from the North Sea to Switzerland – a sort of extended
and inverted version of the *trace Italienne*.

The belligerents turned to new weapons in hopes of breaking
the deadlock, with Germany, the foremost scientific and industrial power of Europe, usually in the lead. Scientists and engineers
responded admirably with poison gas, delivered by artillery shell
in the last year of the war; with planes and zepplins as conveyers
of bombs to wage war on civilians; with tanks to roll through
barbed wire and over trenches to revive mobile warfare. These all
failed to be decisive or appeared too late to affect the outcome of
the war.

The fourth year of the war, 1918, was one of desperation for all
belligerents. Russia surrendered and so Germany could shift troops
from the east to the Western Front, but the British naval blockade was
starving the Kaiser's subjects and fresh American troops were debarking in increasing numbers. Time was not a friend to Germany.

General Erich Ludendorf, who was, in part because of his role
in the Liége assault, the de facto military dictator of Germany,
ordered his divisions forward on the the first day of spring, March
21, to smash the Allied armies. He ordered the most amazing can-

---

[27] Robert Graves, *Poems About War* (Wakefield, RI: Moyer Bell, 1997), 79.

non ever made to begin to bombard Paris on March 23. This was an appeal to technology to break the stalemate that technology had created.

Officers in command of the big naval guns on the Western Front had, months before, asked Ludendorf to approve the building of a cannon with a range of a hundred and more kilometers, more than the distance between German lines and Paris. (They must have also considered that such a gun could reach England across the Channel too.) He granted their request. They turned to the organization that had produced the Big Berthas, the Krupp Artillery Department. This time the Krupp team had no leisure to produce a truly new weapon, but improvised with parts of the naval guns that were available.

The final product, officially called by the Germans *Wilhelm Geschutz* (William's Gun) for the Kaiser, by the French and others Big Bertha (no reason to drop a good name), and by many then and now as simply the Paris Gun, was one of the heaviest ever constructed, one hundred and forty tons, and certainly the longest. To achieve sufficient muzzle velocity to fling the shell up, over, and far beyond the trenches to Paris, the fiery gases of the explosive charge had to be confined behind the accelerating missile for a long time, – that is, the barrel had to be very long. The gun-founders fitted two rifled naval cannon barrels together and then screwed a smooth-bore tube on the end. The total length was 112 feet (34 meters). The barrel was so long and so heavy that it slumped and required a special system of braces. When the cannon was fired, the barrel would buck for an entire minute.

The first shell fired per barrel was twenty-one centimeters in caliber. The friction of its passage and the immense corrosion of the hot gases stripped the lining of the barrel, and so succeeding shells were, one after another, of successively greater calibers so as to fit the eroding barrel. After sixty-five firings, the barrel had to be retired to be rebored.

The first shell only weighed about 260 pounds (120 kilograms),[28] not much compared to the 1,800 pounds (820 kilograms) of the Big Berthas that demolished the Liège forts, but they were not supposed to literally demolish the French army or even Paris, but to bruise and break French morale. They were a psychological, a glamour, almost a magic weapon of which there were to be more in the next world war.

The Paris Gun fired its first shell from a forest near Laon at 7:15 in the morning of March 23. It exited the barrel at an angle of fifty-five degrees so that the missile, slowed by air resistance, would be at forty-five degrees, assuring maximum range, when it emerged into the stratosphere. It rose to an altitude of about 24 miles (40 kilometers), arced through the near vacuum of near space, and descended to explode in front of Number 6 Quai de la Seine in the 19th arrondissement 87.6 miles (140 kilometers) away as measured along the curvature of the earth, 67.7 miles (108 kilometers) as measured in a straight line though the crust of the planet. Never before had humans thrown anything that high or that far.

The gunners were so far from their targets that not only could they not hear the screams of their victims – that milestone had been passed with the trebuchet – they could not even hear the explosions of the shells they fired. The technology of the Paris Gun rendered empathy in war an exercise in abstraction, a challenge for all but the Newtons and Einsteins of morality.

The shells continued to fall on Paris at approximately fifteen-minute intervals that first day, twenty-one of them, killing fifteen and wounding thirty-six. This cannon, soon joined by several other like it, maintained, with two long pauses, a bombardment on the French capital that lasted from March 23 to August 9. A total of 303 shells hit Paris and its suburbs, killing 256 and wounding 620.

---

[28] The shells fired later in the history of a given barrel and in the history of the campaign were progressively heavier.

The Paris Gun altered the course of the war not at all.[29] As the Germans retreated in the fall of 1918 they took the Paris Guns with them or destroyed them. The Allied Disarmament Commission never found any of them in whole or part.[30] The German maestros of projectile technology weren't through.

[29] *Marshall Cavendish Illustrated Encyclopedia of World War I* (New York: Marshall Cavendish, 1984), Vol. 9, 2704–9; Hogg, *Guns, 1914–18*, 134–40.
[30] Ian V. Hogg, *German Secret Weapons of the Second World War* (London: Greenhill Books, 1999), 152.

The Third Acceleration:
Into Extraterrestrial and
Subatomic Space

World War I killed, at conservative estimate, ten million and replaced a discredited and decrepit balance of power system with something worse that seesawed for less than a generation before it fell apart. The French child who was born the day the first shell from the Paris gun exploded in front of Number 6 Quai de la Seine was not old enough to be conscripted into the army when Hitler came to power in Germany.

World War II was several times over more bloody than the first because it was, with the ascent of China and Japan from minor to major roles, more truly a world war, because genocidal monsters had replaced the old emperors in Germany and Russia, and because the ability of humanity to throw fire sprang ahead exponentially between 1939 and 1945.

Combatants on the ground triggered instant firestick holocausts with improved artillery, flame-throwers, and napalm. Airplanes, as many as a thousand at a time, flew over cities to loose deluges of bombs. Humanity sent rockets with warheads of ammonium nitrate and TNT into space to fall on European cities and demolished two Japanese cities with one atomic bomb each. As the war ended, the *Homo sapiens* species was capable of space travel, suicide, and immortality.

NINE

The V-2 and the Bomb

Beyond its invisibility, beyond hammerfall and doomcrack, here is its real horror mocking, promising him death with German and precise confidence...

Thomas Pynchon (1973)[1]

Once the rockets are up, who cares where they come down? "That's not my department," says Wernher von Braun.

Tom Lehrer (1965)[2]

What was gunpowder? Trivial. What was electricity? Meaningless. This Atomic Bomb is the Second Coming in Wrath!

Winston Churchill (1945)[3]

---

[1] Thomas Pynchon, *Gravity's Rainbow* (New York: Penguin Books, 1987), 25.
[2] Tom Lehrer, *Too Many Songs by Tom Lehrer and Not Enough Drawings by Ronald Searle* (New York: Pantheon Books, 1981), 125, 142.
[3] John Keegan, *A History of Warfare* (New York: Alfred A. Knopf, 1993), 379.

The most spectacular advances in projectile technology in World War II were Hitler's *Vergeltungswaffen* (Vengeance Weapons). These were, according to German designation, the V-1 or flying bomb; the V-2, the first long-range rocket; and the V-3, the High-Pressure Pump Gun. These we will consider not in that order, but in the ascending order of their significance for the future of life on earth and, possibly, elsewhere.

Hitler's military experience in practical fact was limited to the Western Front during World War I, a battlefield more dominated by artillery than any before or after. He was, therefore, an easy mark for those who promised Paris Guns good enough to be London guns. And he was *der Führer,* an absolute autocrat free not to listen to what he didn't want to hear.

In 1943 August Coenders of the Röchling Iron and Steelworks proposed to Hitler a better kind of cannon, later titled the V-3. It would, he said, fire shells from the French coast all the way into the heart of London. The barrel would be smooth bore and extremely long, 150 meters, and so would be laid out on natural slopes and ramps, or in slanted tunnels. There would be a number of explosive charges to drive the shell, the first where you would expect, at the lower end of the barrel, and others in chambers along its length. As the shell ascended, these secondary charges would serially detonate behind it, thrusting it from the muzzle at a velocity enormous enough to send it into the vacuum of space and 160 kilometers to the British capital. Fifty of these guns, firing a rate of a round per barrel per minute, would deluge London with explosives, shatter British morale, and win the war.[4]

Hitler approved the construction of an enormous bunker at Mimoyecques near Calais, France, with ten batteries of these High-

---

[4] Dieter Hölsken, *V-Missiles of the Third Reich: The V-1 and V-2* (Sturbridges MA: Monogram Aviation Publications, 1994), 76; Ian V. Hogg, *German Secret Weapons of the Second World War* (London: Greenhill Books, 1999), 45.

Pressure Pump Guns, five per battery, carefully aligned to aim exactly at London. The shafts for these were excavated deep in limestone with a five-meter lid of concrete and steel on top and only the muzzles exposed. The work began in August 1943, employing over 5,000 men. All this took place before adequate testing of the gun or the shells, of which at least 25,000 were manufactured.

In tests, conducted elsewhere, the shells didn't go as far as expected, the V-3 barrels burst again and again, and the several charges per barrel often failed to fire when needed and in proper sequence. And, as you might expect, construction of the bunker lagged and faltered in the confusion of priorities during the run up to the Normandy invasion.

Aerial photo reconnaisance informed the Allies that something ominous was under way at Mimoyecques. They bombed the site over and over, most effectively with twelve-ton "Tallboy" bombs. On July 6, 1944 alone the Royal Air Force dropped almost 2,000 tons of bombs on the bunker. In the same month an American B24 bomber, stripped down and crammed with explosives, took off from England to fly to Mimoyecques and crash into the bunker and detonate. There were two men aboard to tend the plane and then, just before its final dive, to parachute to safety. The plane exploded prematurely, killing them both. One of them, Joseph Kennedy, was the older brother of the future president of the United States. In August Allied forces occupied the Mimoyecques and the high-pressure pump fiasco ended.[5]

The project was absurd. The gun was months, perhaps years, short of being functional. If it had worked, the Allies would have immediately pulverized its site by air, by commando raid, by whatever means required. Londoners would have evacuated, leaving the Mimoyecques guns, which could not be aimed at new targets with-

---

[5] Hölsken, *V-Missiles*, 101, 177–8, 204; David Irving, *The Mare's Nest* (Boston: Little, Brown and Co., 1964), 7, 121, 213–15.

out new excavation and construction, to pound an empty city. And if the shells had poured down, the British people, like the Germans suffering one thousand plane raids, would simply have gritted their teeth and endured.

In contrast to Hitler's high-pressure bombard, Mehemed II's bombards could be re-aimed and the inhabitants of Constantinople were locked into their city as permanent targets. Mehemed II was a sensible megalomaniac. Hitler was not.

The British were anxious to demolish the Mimoyecque bunker, with its racks of bizarre cannons aimed at London. Charles de Gaulle, a student of French history who remembered Joan of Arc and perhaps Maître Jean Bureau too, was slow to agree, so the British went ahead unilaterally, detonating tons of explosives to seal the bunker's entrances and all openings to the outside forever. Behind and below the rubble, in the words of David Irving, historian of the V-weapons, the "subterranean workings of Adolph Hitler's extraordinary 'high-pressure pump' project, complete with steelwork, railways, and high-speed ammunition-lifts, remain to this day, and will endure, no doubt, to perplex the archaeologists of some future age."[6]

The V-3, the High-Pressure Pump Gun, was a flower (if that is the right word) of the artillerists' conception of projectile technology.[7] The V-1 was the product of aviators' concepts. The V-1, also known as the flying bomb, the buzz bomb, and the doodlebug, was the

[6] Irving, *Mare's Nest*, 249–50.
[7] And that, one would think, is the end of that, but right before the Persian Gulf War Iraq was building a giant cannon, either an orthodox monster bigger than the Paris Gun or something along the lines of the High-Pressure Pump Gun. See John Maddox, "Who Wants a Big Gun, and Why?" *Nature*, Vol. 344 (26 April 1990), 811. A part of it is on display at the Royal Artillery Museum in London.

Luftwaffe's solution to the problem of hitting the enemy far beyond the battlefront without losing expensive bombers and crews. It was an unmanned plane – pilots were the most expensive of all aviational components – small and cheap, made mostly of sheet steel, with a simple magnetic and gyroscopic guidance system and a crude timing device to cut the engine over the target, sending the craft, with warhead, plunging down. Its engine, a sort of a pulse jet, was inelegant, but it worked. It had a combustion chamber with flaps on the front that the wind created by the forward movement of the aircraft snapped open. Then low-octane petrol sprayed in to mix with the air and a simple sparkplug ignited the mixture. The explosion slammed the flaps shut and shot out the back, propelling the craft forward. Then wind pressure opened the flaps again and the cycle repeated. The engine sounded like a car with a bad muffler, hence the name buzz bomb. It flew as fast or faster than any planes that might intercept it. It flew day or night, clouds or no clouds.

Its disadvantages were that it had to be traveling at least 190 miles (300 kilometers) an hour before its pulse engine would function and so had to be catapulted off some sort of ramp or taken aloft to be dropped by a bigger and manned plane. The ramps from which most of the V-1s were launched were easy to see from the air and to bomb and strafe. The buzz bomb flew in a straight line, which made it an easy target. Its engine needed lots of air, and so its maximum altitude was 7,000 feet (2,300 meters) and it functioned best at about half that, down where interceptor planes and antiaircraft artillery could easily reach it. The engine and directional equipment were flakey: some V-1's never got airborne and many wandered far off target.[8]

The Germans launched the first V-1's against England on June 13, 1944, a week after the Normandy invasion. The first few

---

[8] Hogg, *German Secret Weapons of the Second World War*, 17–18; Irving, *Mare's Nest*, 239.

hundred to cross the Channel easily penetrated the Allies' defenses, but they soon devised means to defend London and then Antwerp, their chief port on the continent in the last months of the war. Radar, massed antiaircraft guns, proximity fuses, interceptor aircraft stripped for speed, and barrage balloons got most of the buzz bombs.

Antwerp suffered more direct hits than London, but the statistics for the latter are better (not surprisingly, considering the Belgian city's proximity to the battlefront) and suffice as an indication of the effectiveness of the buzz bombs. About 8,000 were launched at England. About 5,400 got through, killing 6,184 and injuring over 17,000 civilians. Its chief value to the German cause was that it obliged the Allies to divert planes and guns from battering the German armed forces, transportation, and industry to fighting off the flying bomb.[9]

The V-1 was the product of aeronautical thinking that rose above the mud of battlefields into the clouds. The V-2 was the product of the imaginings of scientists and seers that soared above the clouds and into the void of space. For them war confirmed that they should do what they passionately wanted to: make big rockets.

Actual use of rockets, except for entertainment and rescue work, had sunk to a nadir in the later nineteenth and early twentieth century. They were used for signaling and illumination during World War I and little more. The victorious statesmen and generals considered them so unimportant that the Versailles Treaty, while it prohibited the German army from having heavy artillery, said nothing about rockets.

---

[9] Winston S. Churchill, *The Second World War: Triumph and Tragedy* (Boston: Houghton Mifflin Co., 1953), 48–9; Peter P. Wegener, *The Peenemünde Wind Tunnels: A Memoir* (New Haven, CT: Yale University Press, 1996), 163.

As the generals, admirals, and prime ministers had lost interest in rockets, the only practical means of willful locomotion in a vacuum, popular interest in space travel increased. In 1865 Jules Verne dispatched fictional characters to the Moon. A generation later H. G. Wells imagined Martians invading Earth. Lesser authors like Edgar Rice Burroughs sent heroes by the dozen whizzing to and fro, left and right, across the solar system. Space travel became a standard condiment of popular culture.[10]

Strange and wonderful children like Konstantin Eduardovich Tsiokovsky, a Russian; Hermann Oberth, a Romanian of German family; and Robert H. Goddard, a Yankee, devoured Verne's tales. Goddard was so deeply affected by H. G. Wells's "War of the Worlds" that he had what in another context might have been called a religious experience. While climbing in a cherry tree on October 19, 1899, he had a dream of traveling to Mars, a vision so poignant that he celebrated its anniversary every year after.

In 1903 Tsiokovsky, who was a quarter-century older than Goddard, published part one of his carefully reasoned, informed, and startling *Exploring Space with Reactive Devices* [i.e., rockets]. He wrote, as the Wright brothers were trying to get their planes off the ground for the first time,

> My mathematical conclusions, based on scientific data verified many times over, show that with such devices [rockets] it is possible to ascend into the expanse of the heavens, and perhaps to found a settlement beyond the limits of the earth's atmosphere ... People will take advantage of this to resettle not only all over the face of the earth but all over the face of the universe.[11]

---

[10] Marjorie Hope Nicolson, *Voyages to the Moon* (New York: Macmillan, 1948), 245–8.

[11] Frank H. Winter, *Rockets into Space* (Cambridge: Harvard University Press, 1990), 7–12; Evgeny Riabchikov, *Russians in Space*, trans. Guy Daniels (Garden City, NY: Doubleday and Co., 1971), 91–103.

Oberth, born in 1894 and the youngest of the three, read Verne's *From the Earth to the Moon* over and over, but not naively. He calculated while a teenager that the instant acceleration of Verne's means to getting people to the moon, a cannon, would subject passengers to a multiplication of their weight by 23,000 times over (we would say 23,000 Gs), mashing them flat. In 1912 he recommended using, instead of a cannon, a rocket with an engine powered by liquid fuels, which could produce more thrust than solid and could be adjusted in output and even turned off and then on again. He especially recommended liquid oxygen (LOX, as it is commonly known today) as a sort of super-saltpeter indispensable for the very rapid combustion of fuel and for any combustion at all in the airless void.[12] It boils at 183 degrees C (297 degrees F) below zero, which renders it devilishly awkward to deal with, but no matter. Tsiokovsky had been thinking along the same line for a long time, and Goddard would be doing so soon.

On March 16, 1926, Goddard launched the world's first successful liquid-fuel rocket at his Aunt Effie's farm in Auburn, Massachusetts. He imagined that it was saying to him, "I've been here long enough; I think I'll be going somewhere else, if you don't mind." The thing was a bit over three meters (ten feet) long and five kilograms (eleven pounds) in weight. The contraption, which looked like a frame for supporting an ailing sapling, rose to treetop height and flew for two and a half seconds, not even so long as the Wright brothers' first aircraft.[13] His triumph went unnoted, as did, for the most part, his experiments later with bigger liquid-fuel rockets. He was in the wrong place at the wrong time.

---

[12] Boris V. Rauschenbach, *Herman Oberth: The Father of Space Flight, 1894–1989,* trans. Lynne Kvinnesland (New York: West Art, 1994), 20–2, 28–9.

[13] Frank H. Winter, *Rockets into Space* (Cambridge: Harvard University Press, 1990), 31; William E. Burrows, *This New Ocean: The Story of the First Space Age* (New York: Random House, 1998), 53–4.

At the beginning of the new century there was no community of those concerned with vehicles for traveling in space – Goddard, Oberth, and Tsiokovsky knew nothing of each other for years – but such began to germinate after World War I. Societies of science fiction and rocket enthusiasts, leavened with a few scientists and engineers, appeared in the Soviet Union, the United States, and elsewhere, most significantly in Germany.

Defeat in World War I shook Germany, releasing all sorts of energies that the old monarchy and establishment had been able to contain. In the 1920s the Bauhaus architects and artists amazed and fascinated, and Bertolt Brecht and Kurt Weill shocked. So did Herman Oberth, the Romanian-German rocket seer, whose doctoral dissertation on astronomy was rejected by the University of Heidelberg for not really being about astronomy. He published it in 1923 as *The Rocket into Planetary Space*. It was the most detailed work yet on the subject, meticulously reasoned, buttressed with pages of mathematics, and it aroused great interest. That year was also the year of Hitler's beer-hall *Putsch*, evidence of another trend that would influence the reach into space.

At the end of the 1920s Germany had a club and a journal devoted to space travel. Oberth brought out an expanded version of his book, of which one young enthusiast, Wernher von Braun, memorized whole passages. Another of Oberth's disciples, Max Valier, published a best seller, *Journey into Outer Space*.

Rocket science, sputtering for lack of its oxidant, money, veered toward theatricality. Oberth contracted with the movie director Fritz Lang to participate in the making of a film, *The Woman on the Moon*. Oberth was supposed to assure its scientific accuracy and to produce a liquid-fuel rocket that would fly to an altitude of fifty kilometers to advertise the film.[14]

[14] Rauschenbach, *Herman Oberth*, 43, 48, 63–5, 97.

Obereth and his colleagues, though they were working on rocket engines for cars and boats as well as flying vehicles – the explosion of one killed Valier – never produced a rocket that climbed to fifty kilometers for the movie's premiere. No one could have at that time. The experts had the theory of space travel down pat, that is, what velocity was required to get into orbit, to escape earthly gravity, and so on, but hadn't the technology and experience of applying that technology to specific engines and vehicles.

The challenges of building a liquid-fuel rocket were daunting to all but fanatics, especially a rocket big enough to carry heavy freight a long way to a precise destination – people, for instance, or a worthwhile quantity of explosive, if you were interested in that sort of payload. Such a vehicle would have to contain as fuel the combustibles of a very large bomb, which would have to combust not all at once but stintingly over a period of, probably, several minutes. The combustion would be not enough to burn through most kinds of metal sheeting and would be in the immediate vicinity of additional combustible fluid. This vehicle would be something like a giant stick of dynamite that would explode decorously from the rear and propel but not damage the freight at the front.

It would travel through the palpable air at enormous speed, which would be likely to produce violent vibration of a vehicle that would not be solid, like a bullet, but a thing of pumps and tubes and tanks and chambers within which flowings and combustions and other measured processes essential to the rocket's functions were happening. There would have to be delicate instruments like a compass and gyroscopes on board, which would, along with everything else, be booming along at several times the speed of sound. During that instrumental trauma, the rocket's weight and distribution thereof would change radically as it consumed its fuel.

The creation of a large, liquid-fuel rocket would require hundreds of scientists and engineers, thousands of workers, and several times over as many marks, rubles, dollars (choose any familiar currency) as the number of kilometers or miles between the earth and the nearest obvious destination for rocket travel, the Moon. No individual or business corporation or society of enthusiasts, however wealthy, had that much money to spend, particularly in the 1930s as humanity tipped into the abyss of the Great Depression. Only governments could foot such a bill.

Karl Emil Becker, an ultranationalist and later a general, was in 1929 a lieutenant colonel in the Ordnance Office of the German Army. He had participated in the Paris Gun operation in 1918, a tour of duty that taught him that the missiles fired from that cannon went as far as they did not simply because of the charge that drove them per se, but because it drove them so high that they traveled most of the distance to target above the atmosphere. His faith – there is no better word for this – was that a new and better glamour weapon, one propelling a bigger missile higher and therefore farther, would smash enemy morale and win wars. He also knew that the Versailles Treaty forbid the German Army heavy artillery, but passed over rocketry.[15]

In 1929 the Reich Defense Ministry approved Becker's plan for a small rocket program. He began to gather the most promising among the rocket enthusiasts, civilian and military. Oberth had run out of money and returned to Romania, and was perhaps too purely a theorist anyway. Captain (in time a general) Walter R. Dornberger, a ballistics expert, also a veteran artillerist of the war, was Becker's most valuable early recruit. He could talk to the theorists and engineers in their own terms, and would prove to be indefatigable during the coming rivalry with the Luftwaffe and all other rivals for funds, personnel, and materials. Becker's orders to him were simple – "You have to develop a liquid rocket which can

[15] Michael J. Neufeld, *The Rocket and the Reich: Peenemünde and the Coming of the Ballistic Missile Era* (Cambridge: Harvard University Press, 1995), 5–6.

carry more payload than any shell presently in our artillery" – and matched neatly with his own obsessions.[16]

In autumn 1932 Dornberger hired as his first technical assistant, the nineteen-year-old Wernher von Braun. He was a physicist and engineer (not an everyday combination), enough of an aristocrat in ancestry (note the "von") and manner to impress anyone who needed impressing in such matters, and proved to be an effective administrator and a charismatic leader. He was looking for – his words – "a golden cow." He found it in the military, first German and then American.[17]

Dornberger assembled the experts and equipment for a rocket-testing facility at an old firing range at Kummersdorf, not far from Berlin. Braun finished his doctoral dissertation there, "Constructive, Theoretical and Experimental Contributions to the Problem of the Liquid-Fueled Rocket." The University of Berlin accepted it and the government classified it as secret, as it did all rocket research from that time on.[18]

At Kummersdorf a mutual deception of military and space travel enthusiasts ensued. The soldiers wanted super-long range artillery and learned to listen respectfully to the vaporizings of the latter. The latter, who wanted vehicles to go to the Moon and Mars, were equally tolerant, and if soldiers wanted to use their rockets in the meanwhile to carry bombs, well so be it – and space enthusiasts could be patriots too, after all.

In 1934 the Dornberger-von Braun team launched two small experimental liquid-fuel rockets that soared to altitudes of nearly one and a half miles, over two kilometers. Von Braun was already talking

[16] Hölsken, *V-Missiles*, 166; Neufeld, *Rocket and the Reich*, 51; Frank H. Winter, *Rockets into Space* (Cambridge: Harvard University Press, 1990), 46.
[17] Neufeld, *Rocket and the Reich*, 22; Peter P. Wegener, *The Peenemünde Wind Tunnels, A Memoir* (New Haven, CT: Yale University Press, 1996), 161.
[18] Dennis Piszkiewicz, *Wernher von Braun: The Man Who Sold the Moon* (Westport, CT: Praeger, 1998), 28.

of something much larger, a rocket that would weigh 1,650 pounds (750 kilograms) at takeoff. It would be large enough to carry the latest in guidance systems, that is, it could be more than simply a javelin after release from the thrower's hand. Dornberger (in part unknowingly echoing Congreve) was talking of a rocket that could deliver a warhead weighing a ton 160 miles or 100 kilometers.[19] The government, now Nazi, pledged millions of marks for the effort.

The German rocket team needed a site bigger and more remote than Kummersdorf. "Why don't you take a look at Peenemünde," von Braun's mother suggested. "Your grandfather used to go duck-hunting there." Isolated and thinly populated, it faced an open sea and along a coast from which rocket flights could be observed for about 300 miles or 200 kilometers. It was lovely, as well, a Shangri La in which to spend a career with brilliant and congenial colleagues. The German rocket team moved there in the spring of 1937.[20]

The bulk of research that underlies modern liquid-fuel rocketry was accomplished at Peenemünde, which became in size and significance for rocketry what Los Alamos represented for nuclear bomb research. The Nazi government was the only institution in the world at that time willing to pour wealth into rocket after rocket that exploded, that veered off course and crashed, that gave gross evidence of being a waste of money, but that provided data for the next and better rocket.

The challenge presented to the rocketeers was like that of a blacksmith of Napoleon's generation told to build an automobile and presented with a copy of the laws of thermodynamics for guidance and a stagecoach for a model. There were some successes at the beginning, but between 1934 and 1939 every launch at Peenemünde failed. In 1940 Becker committed suicide. According

---

[19] Hölsken, *V-Missiles*, 16–21.
[20] Neufeld, *Rocket and the Reich* 48–9; Hölsken, *V-Missiles*, 22.

to Dornberger, it was after a quarrel with Hitler, who had little appreciation of advanced technology. Peenemünde was producing nothing but failures, and the war was going so well that Hitler decided to cut back on funds for experimental projects.[21]

What kept the German rocketeers going was little more than technological romanticism. "It was like planning a miracle," Albert Speer, Hitler's future Minister of Armaments, wrote later.

In 1942 the Peenemünde team had prototypes of the V-2 ready to test. The first of the monsters soared, faltered, and fell. The second blew up at 35,000 feet. On the third try the Peenemünde team had a piece of luck and a reward for their perseverance. The fourteen-ton, forty-six foot rocket, driven by an engine burning liquid oxygen and alcohol, soared to an altitude of 53 miles (85 kilometers) at a speed of 3,300 miles per hour. Five minutes after launch and 120 miles (190 kilometers) down range the rocket plunged into the Baltic.

The rocket bore the logo *The Woman on the Moon*. The vehicle that Oberth had pledged for Lang's film had finally flown and then some – and Oberth had been lucky enough to be there to see it.[22] He expressed admiration for the rocket's designers, but he was still obsessed with the future: "This rocket is only a small step towards the conquest of outer space."

Dornberger boasted that they had broken the altitude record of "the now almost legendary Paris Gun," and that we have "proved rocket propulsion practicable for space travel." But he found his way back to the present quickly: "So long as the war lasts, our most urgent task can only be the rapid perfecting of the rocket as a weapon." [23]

---

[21] Walter Dornberger, *V2*, trans. James Cleugh and Geoffrey Halliday (London; Hurst and Blackett, 1954), 75.

[22] Wegener, *This Peenemünde Wind Tunnels*, 162; Piszkiewicz, *Wernher von Braun*, 32–3; 49–50; http://www.wsmr.army.mil/paopage/PAO.htm.

[23] William E. Burrows, *The New Ocean: The Story of the First Space Age* (New York: Random House, 1998), 99–100; Rauschenbach, *Hermann Oberth*, 119; Piszkiewicz, *Wernher von Braun*, 33; Dornberger, *V2*, 29.

The Peenemünde team returned to informative failures. The V-2 prototypes were unpredictable in navigation and often broke apart on reentry into the atmosphere. But, fortunately for these rocketeers, events were beginning to turn against Germany. The Soviet Union was refusing to accept clear proof that it was defeated and now the United States was in the war. Dismay stimulated Hitler to reach for miracles, to increase support for the V-2 program.

As the Peenemünde team, by now numbering thousands of Germans and hundreds of foreign workers, labored to make the V-2 operational, the Allies tardily took note of what was happening there. On the night of August 18–19, 1943, nearly 500 bombers converged over Peenemünde and, if they failed to hit many of the specific targets as planned, did kill hundreds, smashed housing, and made it obvious that the rocket facility was vulnerable. In September the rocket was ready for deployment, but the bombers were sure to return to Peenemünde. Hitler ordered the production of the V-2 shifted to Mittelwerk, an underground factory complex in the Hartz Mountains. The move slowed the production and deployment of the V-2s by weeks, and the first were not launched on enemy targets until September 1944.[24]

The elite corps of the Nazi party, the SS, ran Mittelwerk, which was staffed with slave laborers. Of the approximately 60,000 workers who passed through the Mittelwerk system, 20,000 died. About half of those who did not survive were involved in producing V-2s. The rockets grew in a garden of horrors.[25]

The advantages of the V-2 over the Paris Gun lay, first, in its relative maneuverability. The cannon and its carriage weighed far over a hundred tons, and moving it can be accurately compared to

[24] Irving, *Mare's Nest*, 135, 300; Hogg, *German Secret Weapons*, 43.
[25] Neufeld, *The Rocket and the Reich*, 264. See also Yves Béon, *Planet Dora: A Memoir of the Holocaust and the Birth of the Space Age*, trans. Rihard L. Fague (Boulder, CO: Westview Press, 1998).

moving a house. The V-2 was by no means compact, but it could be trucked into position in hours, launched soon after, and then everything packed up for the move to the next site in another few hours. Its greatest strength compared to any cannon was in the weight of its payload. Four V-2s carried in total as much explosive as all the shells fired on Paris by the Paris Gun.[26]

Its advantages over the V-1 were that it needed no elaborate ramp. Another was its speed: no V-2 was ever shot down by interceptor or artillery. Indeed, it traveled so fast that the sound wave it caused arrived after it did. Its relative disadvantages were that it was too complicated, a finicky thoroughbred compared to the mongrel V-1, and much more expensive to produce in terms of time, skill, and money.

On September 6, 1944, the first one was launched at Paris, not London, the target for which it had been designed. (One wonders if the target picker was somehow expressing a fond recollection of the Paris Gun.) Then, on September 8, the first V-2 destined for London went on its way. All in all, about 4,000 were launched, more on Antwerp than London because Allied armies soon pushed the Germans out of the areas from which the rocket could reach the British capital.[27]

Twenty-five percent of the V-2s failed in the air and only the lucky ones hit even targets as big as the downtowns and docks they were aimed at. As with the V-1, the most reliable statistics pertaining to the V-2's effectiveness are about those aimed at England. There were 1,000 to 1,300 of them: they injured 6,300 and killed 2,700. These fatalities, plus those the V-2 killed elsewhere, are less

[26] *Marshall Cavendish Illustrated Encyclopedia of World War I*, ed. Peter Young (New York: Marshall Cavendish, 1984), Vol. 9, 2707; V. Hogg, *The Guns 1914–18* (New York: Ballantine Books, 1971), 137.
[27] Winter, *Rockets into Space*, 49–50.

in total than the number of slave workers who died manufacturing the rockets.[28]

The last V-2 launched to kill left the ground on March 27, 1945.[29] Nazi Germany surrendered unconditionally on May 7, 1945. On the same day, scientists and technicians of the Allied powers exploded a stack of one hundred tons of high explosives in the southwestern desert of the United States. That was the biggest intentional chemical explosion in the history of the world. It was detonated to test instruments installed there to evaluate an explosion to take place shortly after that would be almost two hundred times greater.[30]

The V-2 did not change the outcome of World War II because the Germans had no explosive worthy of it, that is, one powerful enough to mortally wound a city with a near miss. Hitler crooned of a rocket carrying ten tons of explosive to Dornberger, who held his tongue. No such rocket existed or could for years, and, anyway, even ten-ton warheads of current explosives could not win the war for Germany. He daydreamed about some sort of atomic energy warhead, an idle dream for those who served Hitler.[31]

In the middle decades of the nineteenth century the science of physics had seemed almost as cut and dried as the rules of arithmetic.

---

[28] Wegener, *The Peenemünde Wind Tunnels* 163; Neufeld, *The Rocket and the Reich,* 264.; Frederick I. Ordway III and Mitchell R. Sharpe, *The Rocket Team: From the V-2 to the Saturn Moon Rocket* (New York: Thomas Y. Crowell, 1979), 79.

[29] Hogg, *German Secret Weapons,* 43.

[30] Richard Rhodes, *The Making of the Atomic Bomb* (New York: Simon and Schuster, 1986), 654; Vincent C. Jones, *United States Army in World War II, Special Studies, Manhattan, the Army and the Atomic Bomb* (Washington, DC: Center of Military History, United States Army, 1985), 512.

[31] Dornberger, V2, 106.

Common sense had seemed a dependable guide for consideration of physical reality. Matter and energy were, for physicists as for plumbers, very different things. Time and space ticked and measured the same everywhere and under every condition. Atoms were like tiny billiard balls and performed like them. James Clerk Maxwell, founder of the Cavendish Laboratory at the University of Cambridge, proclaimed that atoms "continue this day as they were created – perfect in number and measure and weight."[32]

Albert Michelson, America's superb experimentalist, announced in 1894 that "it seems probable that most of the grand underlying principles have been firmly established and that further advances are to be sought chiefly in the rigorous application of these principles to all the phenomenon which comes under our notice."[33] There were admittedly still a few disturbing oddities. Michelson himself had already participated in discovering that the speed of light as measured on the moving Earth seemed to be the same in all directions, which was odd indeed.

Then Röntgen, the Curies, Plank, Rutherford, Einstein, Bohr, and other prophets, warlocks, and witches of a new physics conducted their little experiments and expended a great deal of chalk on blackboards, and the marriage of atomic reality and common sense ended in nasty divorce. Matter and energy became situational; time and space became variables; atoms changed from billiard balls into vacant lots through which quanta of energy scampered and flowed; and Laws of Nature became formulas of probabilities. As Niels Bohr once remarked, "If anyone says he can think about quantum problems without getting giddy, that only shows he had not understood the first thing about them."[34]

[32] Rhodes, *Making of the Atomic Bomb*, 30.
[33] Helge Kragh, *Quantum Generations: A History of Physics in the Twentieth Century* (Princeton: Princeton University Press, 1999), 3.
[34] Rhodes, *Making of the Atomic Bomb*, 152.

The new physicists were picking the lock of a door beyond which there was unimaginable power, the power of the atom. In 1903, the year the Wright brothers first flew and Tsiokovsky published *Exploring Space with Reactive Devices*, Frederick Soddy, who would later win a Nobel Prize, declared:

> It is probable that all heavy matter possesses – latent and bound up with the structure of the atom – a similar quantity of energy to that possessed by radium. If it could be tapped and controlled what an agent it would be in shaping the world's destiny! The man who put his hand on the lever by which a parsimonious nature regulates jealously the output of this store of energy would possess a weapon by which he could destroy the earth if he chose.[35]

Few scientists paid attention to such extravagant prophesy and fewer laypersons. H. G. Wells, the science fictionist who wrote about such twaddle as space and time travel, did. Darwin had remarked that fire was humanity's greatest invention, barring language. Wells predicted that human harnessing of atomic energy would be equally important.[36]

The experiments and insights that led to the release of nuclear energy for human purposes, destructive and constructive, tumbled one after the other in the years after the last Paris Gun disappeared. The challenge was to find some projectile that could pierce the atom's ramparts of electric charges and plunge into and disrupt the balances within the nucleus, with informative results that might revolutionize atomic physics. That projectile turned out to be the neutron, a particle with the blunderbuss mass of a proton

---

35 Rhodes, *The Making of the Atomic Bomb*, 44.
36 Charles Darwin, *The Origin of Species and the Descent of Man* (New York: The Modern Library, n.d.), 432; H. G. Wells, *The World Set Free: A Story of Mankind* (New York: E. P. Dutton, 1914), passim.

and no charge at all to provoke rejection – a *neut*-ron. Its discovery was completed by James Chadwick in 1932, who thus earned himself a Nobel.[37]

Adolph Hitler came to power in 1933 and five years after that Otto Hahn and Fritz Strassmann bombarded a tiny sample of uranium with neutrons, accomplishing something wonderful and mysterious: the first intentional and unambiguous example of atomic fission.[38] Their laboratory was in Berlin. World War II began the next year.

At the beginning of the 1930s a great many, a plurality arguably, of the best quantum physicists in the world were German. If Hitler had fully exploited the scientific potential of the society he rose to dominate, he would have exceeded many times over the horrors he did commit.

He did exploit his rocketeers, if tardily, as we have seen. To understand what they envisioned did not absolutely require a grasp of higher mathematics or the insights of a mystic. And his rocketeers, unlike his physicists, were all Aryans.

"Hitler had sometimes spoken to me about the possibility of an atom bomb," Albert Speer, wrote after the war, "but the idea obviously strained his intellectual capacity. He was also unable to grasp the revolutionary nature of nuclear physics."[39] His pathological intolerance for Jews reinforced his disbelief in nuclear research.[40]

Mehemed II had surely detested Christians' faith, but not their ancestry. Most of his Janissaries were of Christian birth and Urban, his bombardier, likewise, but he overlooked that and asked of them nothing more than to obey his every wish. He might

---

[37] Kragh, *Quantum Generations,* 184–5.
[38] Kragh, *Quantum Generations,* 257–60.
[39] Rhodes, *The Making of the Atomic Bomb,* 404–5.
[40] The full story can be found in Jean Medawar and David Pyke, *Hitler's Gift: Scientists Who Fled Nazi Germany* (London: Richard Cohen Books, 2000).

require Christians to convert to Islam, but not to cease to exist. Hitler was less of a pragmatist, more of an absolutist. When Max Plank once suggested to him – oh, so gently – that dismissing Jewish scientists would weaken the Reich, he answered that if their explusion "means the annihilation of contemporary German science, then we shall do without science for a few years!"

Aryan physics, in contrast to Jewish (i.e., quantum) physics was based on commonsensical theory and experiments with visualizable results. Its proponents failed Hitler, as did the quantum physicists who stayed home to work for the Third Reich – Plank, Heisenberg, Hahn, and a few others. Nuclear physics withered in what a different kind of a German patriot than Hitler might have jingoistically claimed as its homeland.[41]

Twenty-five percent of the physics community that existed in Germany when Hitler came to power went into exile, among them six Nobel laureates. Of the nation's sixty university teachers with positions in theoretical physics, twenty-six left. Most were at least in part of Jewish ancestry or married to spouses of such origin. Others of similar background in Italy and Hungary and elsewhere in continental Europe also left. They fled in all directions, many to Great Britain, over half to the United States.[42] There they spent every effort to defeat the Nazis.

Their first and perhaps their most significant contribution was a matter not of their knowledge and skill but of their reputations. In 1939 when Hitler, with Stalin as an ally, won all the battles, several immigrant physicists newly arrived in the United States – Leo Szilard, Eugene Wigner, and Edward Teller – drafted a letter to President Franklin Delano Roosevelt, introducing him to the subject of atomic fission, informing him of its military potential, and warning that Germany had probably already begun research on an

[41] Kragh, *Quantum Generations*, 230, 236–8, 271–2.
[42] Kragh, *Quantum Generations*, 230, 231–2, 236–8, 271–2.

Figure 12. Albert Einstein and Leo Szilard, leaders among those who persuaded President Roosevelt to initiate the Manhattan Project. March of Time/TimePix.

atomic bomb. Albert Einstein, another exiled physicist and the most famous scientist alive, signed the letter, and off it went to the White House (Fig. 12).[43]

Roosevelt did not commit the United States to the making of the A-bomb immediately, but smiled on or at least turned a thoughtfully blind eye to small beginnings toward that goal. He needed more evidence, as did many others, including some physicists. Enrico Fermi, another exile, this one from fascist Italy, provided that. In December 1942, under the stands of an old football stadium at the University of Chicago, he directed the assembling of

[43] Kragh, *Quantum Generations*, 265–6; Jones, *United States Army*, 13–15. The complete text of the Einstein–Roosevelt letter can be found in numerous sources, for instance, Medawar and Pyke, *Hitler's Gift*, 218–9.

six tons of uranium metal, thirty-four of uranium oxide, and 385 of grafite (to slow and tame the neutrons) into the world's first atomic pile. It did not melt down in the middle of America's second biggest city and did produce the first solid evidence of a phenomenon indispensable for an atomic bomb, a self-sustaining "chain" reaction. Each collision of neutron with uranium nucleus produced more free neutrons, which collided with other nuclei, producing more free neutrons, and so on and on. Making an atomic bomb was feasible. Shortly after, Roosevelt approved the first $250 million to do so.[44]

That effort was the biggest single research and development project yet in history. The Manhattan Project, as it was code-named, employed 43,000 people at thirty-seven installations across North America, some of them literally secret cities, and cost two billion dollars.[45]

At 5:29.45 on the morning of June 16, 1945, at a location in New Mexico known to Spanish speakers as the *Jornada del Muerto*, a piece of the Sun materialized. Physicists and engineers and technicians of the Manhattan Project detonated chemical explosives (children of the Taoists' gunpowder) to compress a sphere of plutonium to critical mass and trigger a chain reaction. Fermi had cheerfully offered to bet that this would ignite the atmosphere and destroy the world or at least New Mexico. The result was not that, but was an explosion with a force of 18.6 thousand tons of TNT.[46] There was now a bomb worthy of V-2 and its intercontinental children.

✳ ✳ ✳

44 Kragh, *Quantum Generations*, 266–7; Jones *United States Army*, 102–4.
45 James E. McClellan III and Harold Dorn, *Science and Technology in World History* (Baltimore: Johns Hopkins Press, 1999), 361.
46 Rhodes, *The Making of the Atomic Bomb*, 652, 654, 664, 677.

Humanity equipped with atlatl and firestick was instrumental in the elimination of scores of species of megafauna. Now, equipped with long-range rocket and fission bomb (and, in the next decade, with the fusion bomb, with output measured not in kilo- but megatons) was capable of eliminating thousands upon thousands of species, including its own.

TEN

The Longest Throws

Let us create vessels and sails adjusted to the heavenly ether...

Johann Kepler to Galileo Galilei (c. 1600)[1]

Mission Status—22 February 2001
Pioneer 10 distance from Sun: 77.21 AU Speed relative to the Sun: 12.24 km/sec (27,380 mph) Distance from Earth: 11.52 billion kilometers (7.16 billion miles) Round-trip Light Time: 21 hours 20 minutes[2]

Gunpowder made the European nation-states and empires possible, and their rivalries led to the cordite catastrophe of World War I. That led to World War II, a catastrophe so destructive that it exhausted the major powers with one exception, the United States, which emerged with only one possible rival, the Soviet Union. The prospect was that their rivalry would lead to World War III, which, with the weaponry developed in the 1940s, would kill us all.

---

[1] Wyn Wachhorst, "Kepler's Children: The Dreams of Spaceflight," *Yale Review*, Vol. 84 (April 1996), 114.
[2] http://spaceprojects.arc.nasa.gov/Space_Projects/pioneer/PNStat.html.

We were saved from that cataclysm by that very weaponry, the long-range bombers and rockets with their payloads of plutonium and hydrogen devastation. Humans had at long last invented weapons dreadful enough to frighten their makers into at least temporary restraint and sanity. The standoff between the United States and the U.S.S.R was called the Cold War and its logic was called MAD (Mutually Assured Destruction).

Not that the years of the Cold War were peaceful. The two superpowers fought cordite wars by proxy; China completed a century of turmoil and revolution with a Communist victory in 1949; peasant armies turned to guerilla tactics to counter their old rulers' technological advantage and send them packing. In Africa and Asia dozens of independent states arose to succeed the European overseas empires. But the superpowers, like basketball players trying to block each others' shots without direct collision and ensuing penalty, abstained from World War III.

Theirs became a competition for prestige, a popularity contest, if you will. These superpowers struggled and strained to get into space "fustest with the mostest," to quote an old American general. Which was going to dazzle the world with its space prowess and lead the way into its version of earthly salvation?

We will satisfy ourselves with two samples drawn from the record of that context, frankly selected for their sensational qualities. Sensationalism has always figured prominently in projectile technology. In 1969 *Homo sapiens* dispatched two of its number to the Moon; and in 1972 launched a 570-pound (270-kilogram) package to Jupiter and clean out of our solar system.

These were American triumphs because the United States was rich, had come through the war with scientific and industrial infrastructure intact, and was shrewd enough to clasp the Peenemünde team, the most successful rocketeers of the first half of the twentieth century, to its red, white, and blue bosom.

It was customary of old for the victors in war to plunder the losers of their golden candelabras, silver goblets, and women. By 1945 the nature of greed and lust had changed, and the winners of the war in Europe craved the products of German science and technology and the scientists and technicians who could make more of them.

The Peenemünde elite had in their artifacts, knowledge, and skills something with which to bargain for survival and for the realization of their fantasy about space travel. One of them later described their state of mind in the spring of 1945: "We despise the French; we are mortally afraid of the Soviets; we do not believe the British can afford us, so that leaves the Americans."[3]

The Peenemünde elite arranged to be as safe and comfortable as they could manage during the spring Göterdämmerung of 1945 to wait for the Americans to find them. On May 2, 1945, two days after Hitler's suicide, Private First Class Fredrick P. Schneikert of the 44th Infantry Division, armed with an M-1 rifle with the safety off, came upon Magnus von Braun, Wernher's younger brother, out on a bicycle looking for the U.S. Army. A few days later Wernher made a bet with Private Schneikert that he would get to America before the American soldier. The rocketeer won the bet and the next page in the history of space travel turned.[4]

Mehemed II had welcomed Urban because he could make big cannons. The United States welcomed Wernher von Braun and his colleagues because they could make big rockets. "Screen them for being Nazis!" asked one American army lieutenant, too young and insignificant to mince words. "What the hell for?" he answered. "Look, if they were Hitler's brothers, it's beside the point. Their

[3] William E. Burrows, *This New Ocean: The Story of the First Space Age* (New York: Random House, 1998), 108.

[4] Frederick I. Ordway III and Mitchell R. Sharpe, *The Rocket Team: From the V-2 to the Saturn Moon Rocket* (New York: Thomas Y. Crowell, 1979), 1–10.

knowledge is valuable for both military and possible national reasons."[5] That is an argument easier to hold in contempt than to counter.

Like all the major belligerents, the United States had used rockets in the war, most famously bazookas as antitank weapons, but these, like the Russian Katyushas, were short-range weapons. Now that the immediate demands of combat were stilled and German genius was available for exploitation – and the Cold War obviously the next major item on the docket of history – now the victors could indulge their primal urge to cultivate the means to throw big things a long way.

The United States, with all its techno-scientific potential and Robert Goddard on hand, should have led the world in rocket research in the 1930s and 1940s, but neither its elites nor masses were inclined to do so, and Goddard, a man more like Charles Ives than Dale Carnegie, was far from having the kind of personality to mobilize public opinion in his favor. He had not celebrated his 1926 rocket, published little, and discouraged imitators by locking up his inventions with two hundred patents. He was as much a visionary as Oberth or Tsiokovsky, dreaming of interplanetary travel, of escaping to other solar systems before the death of our Sun, but he was the wrong man in the wrong society to recruit many followers.

He attracted some grant money, at least once through the effort of Charles Lindbergh, and went off to launch experimental rockets in a place accurately named High Lonesome in the New Mexican desert. In 1930 one of his flew to 2,000 feet (650 meters) and in 1935 another to 7,500 feet. Historians regard these as major achievements, but they attracted little notice at the time.

He did experimental work on rockets for the U.S. government during World War II, and when, in 1945, the first V-2s arrived in

---

[5] Dennis Piszkiewicz, *Wernher von Braun: The Man Who Sold the Moon* (Westport, CT: Praeger, 1998), 54.

the United States, was among the first to examine one. He worried that the Germans, who knew little of his work, had stolen some of his ideas.

Goddard died of cancer in August 1945 on the day the war ended. Theodor von Karmen, an early German exile and now a professor of aeronautics at the California Institute of Technology (CalTech), wrote of him, "There is no direct line from Goddard to present-day rocketry. He is on a branch that died"[6] – a cruel epitaph and too definitive, but largely true.

The American scientific and technological community of the 1930s and 1940s was not entirely antediluvian vis-à-vis rocketry. There had been an American Rocket Society like the German and some experiments with rockets for high-altitude research. Graduate students and professors at CalTech in Los Angeles were intrigued with rocketry, and conducted experiments in a dry arroyo nearby. Spin-offs from such meager beginnings include the soon world-famous Jet Propulsion Laboratory.

In October 1945, a bit over a month after Goddard died, a 665-pound WAC-Corporal rocket soared from White Sands, New Mexico, not very far from High Lonesome or the spot of the first atomic bomb detonation, to a height of forty-five miles.[7] The American rocket community was well prepared to understand and build on whatever the immigrants from Peenemünde had to teach.[8]

The Germans' advance man, the estimable Wernher von Braun, arrived in Newcastle Army Air Base, Delaware, on September 18, 1945. Hitler was dead six months; Stalin had eight years to go. In the next five months 117 more German rocket scientists arrived in

6 William E. Burrows, *This New Ocean: The Story of the First Space Age* (New York: Random House, 1998), 90–3; T. A. Heppenheimer, *Countdown: A History of Space Flight* (New York: John Wiley & Sons, 1997), 31–3.
7 Frank H. Winter, *Rockets into Space* (Cambridge: Harvard University Press, 1990), 62–3.
8 Heppenheimer, *Countdown*, 46.

the United States. These included, all of V-2 fame, August Schultz, systems engineer; Erich Neuberet of the Electronics, Guidance, and Telemetry Laboratory; Theodor Poppel of the Test Laboratory; and Walter Schwidetzky, instrumentation engineer.[9] Dornberger lagged behind: he had to go through a war crimes trial in Great Britain before he joined his colleages. At first they were, as they wryly called themselves, "prisoners of peace," but in time most of them became citizens of the United States.[10]

The American rocketeers, now augmented by the Germans, had the same visions of space travel as Tsiokovsky, Goddard, and Oberth, and also had the same chronic problem. They needed mountains of money, amounts that only a government could provide. Von Braun had announced to the U.S. Army at first contact in May 1945 that "When the art of rockets is developed further, it will be possible to go to other planets, first of all to the Moon,"[11] but that was not a message the generals and their masters wanted to hear. They wanted weapons against which there would be no defense, especially after Joseph Stalin welded an "iron curtain" across Europe and, with the Berlin Blockade in 1948, seemed to be bullying the world toward obedience or another war.

Ergo, American presidents and senators and representatives shoveled out billions upon billions for defense, for Intercontinental Ballistic Missiles (ICBMs) capable of hitting Kiev from Kansas, for rockets to put satellites into the sky to peer down on the Soviet Union from the edge of space.

The United States began its drive to produce long-range rockets with, as William E. Burrows has put it, a "starter set" of German rocket scientists, 360 tons of V-2 components (some or most of

[9] Piszkiewicz, *Wernher von Braun*, 5, 9; Ordway and Sharpe, *Rocket Team*, 310.
[10] For the full story of this migration, see Clarence G. Lasby, *Project Paperclip: German Scientists and the Cold War* (New York: Atheneum, 1971).
[11] Ordway and Sharpe, *Rocket Team*, 271.

which had been made by Mittelwerk slaves), and fourteen tons or so of Peenemünde documents, including, for instance, 510,000 engineering drawings. Between April 16, 1946, and September 19, 1952, the Germans and their American acolytes launched sixty-seven V-2s in New Mexico. Until 1957 America's big rockets (and Russia's too) were really no more than upgraded versions of the V-2 and, even after that, as we shall see, the German element in the American space effort remained important.[12]

Both the United States and the Soviet Union built up stockpiles of liquid fuel and then solid fuel intermediate-range ballistic missiles (IRBMs) and intercontinental ballistic missiles (ICBMs). These giant rockets were what the space travel fanciers needed to implement their plans, but getting the use of them for their Jules Vernian schemes wasn't easy. To promote that conversion they had to do more than to scare their patrons: they had to enlist them in a crusade.

They had in their midst a master promotionist, Wernher von Braun, who after a few years in the United States turned to his colleague, Dr. Adolph K. Thiel, and said in purest American idiom, "We can dream about rockets and the Moon until Hell freezes over. Unless the *people* understand it and the man who pays the bill is behind it, no dice. You worry about your damned calculations, and I'll talk to the people."[13]

The amazing Wernher von Braun had begun life as a Junker aristocrat, had worked in utter secrecy as a brilliant rocket engineer and administrator to the benefit of one of the most dictatorial and secretive regimes of all history, and then tap-danced across the Atlantic to become, again, a brilliant rocket engineer and administrator, and this time a celebrity in a democratic and publicity-mad

[12] Burrows, *This New Ocean.* 119–23, 132; Heppenheimer, *Countdown,* 116; Ordway and Sharpe, *Rocket Team,* 314.
[13] Ordway and Sharpe, *Rocket Team,* 361.

society. He was what Goddard wasn't – a rocketeer with a talent for persuasion. He had exploited the Nazis to get started on the road to the Moon and now would do so with the Republicans and Democrats by appealing to American patriotism, paranoia, triumphalism, and always to the subliminal yearning for the Long Throw.

In January 1947 von Braun began his career as rocketry's master of ceremonies with a speech to the Rotary Club of El Paso, Texas, an unlikely mise-en-scène for a man of his background and interests. His speech included the themes he would play on for the rest of his life. He proposed an enlarged V-2 as a spaceship; he proposed a three-state rocket to put a satellite into orbit; he proposed a winged rocket to launch beyond the atmosphere and return and land like a airplane; he proposed a space station from which to launch flights to the Moon and planets.[14]

The Rotarians probably didn't understand half of what he said and may have thought the other half science fiction fantasy, but they and millions of Americans like them were preadapted to learn. They were citizens of the homeland of the Wright brothers and Lindbergh, a land where the Long Throw – the home run, the Hail Mary pass – was sacred.

In 1952 von Braun collaborated on a series of articles, stunningly illustrated, on space travel in one of America's most widely read magazines, *Collier's*, a publicity triumph. He went on to collaborate with Walt Disney to provide the master popularizer's television series with programs with titles like "Rocket to the Moon" and to construct a space travel component for one of Disney's theme parks (Fig. 13).

The Eisenhower presidency closed amid jeremiads about the missile gap. The United States was decisively ahead of the Soviet Union in bombers, but the bomber was no longer the deus ex

---

[14] Piszkiewicz, *Wernher von Braun*, 15.

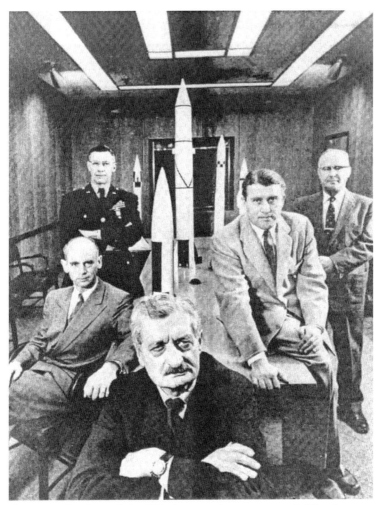

Figure 13. Leaders of the U.S. Army rocket team, 1956. Wernher von Braun, right center, and Hermann Oberth, foreground, loom largest, as is fitting. NASA.

machina de rigueur. In October 1957 the Russians launched *Sputnik,* the first artificial satellite, into orbit. America's attempt to do the same via its Vanguard rocket ended in gross embarrassment as the rocket blew up – on camera. Not until the following January did Von Braun and the multistage Jupiter rocket, with a Redstone, an elongated version of the V-2, as the first-stage booster, come to the rescue and put an American satellite, tiny but at least *up* there, into orbit.[15] The Soviet's Yuri Gagarin soared into orbit around the earth in April 1961. The United State's John Glenn didn't follow until February a year later. The Soviets seemed to always be first, the Americans second.

Lyndon Baynes Johnson, at the end of the 1950s the most powerful man in the U.S. Senate, raved like an Old Testament prophet: "From space the masters of infinity would have the power to control the earth's weather, to cause drought and flood, to change the tides and raise the levels of the sea, to divert the Gulf Stream and change temperate climates to frigid."[16]

The United States retained its lead in powers of destruction over the Soviet Union, but not in its own or the world's perception. American morale was tumbling and its international leadership in doubt. President John F. Kennedy decided to choose a goal so spectacular that achieving it would dwarf all the Soviet triumphs. On May 25, 1961, he announced before a joint session of Congress and to the world that "this nation should commit itself to achieving the goal, before this decade is out, of landing a man on the moon and returning him safely to earth." This, the longest throw yet, would be the publicity coup of the century – if not botched like the Vanguard launch.

Building the moon rocket, soon christened the *Saturn,* became the top priority of NASA (National Aeronautics and Space

---

[15] Piszkiewicz, *Wernher von Braun,* 115–20.
[16] Heppenheimer, *Countdown,* 126.

THROWING FIRE

182

Administration), with von Braun in charge of the production of its big boosters and other Germans among his lieutenants. He succeeded as administrator and publicist and they accomplished the task on schedule.[17]

The *Saturn V*, completed by 1968, was a three-stage rocket 364 feet tall, that is, it was an entity designed to fly that was taller than a thirty-story building and sixty feet taller than the Statue of Liberty on its pedestal. It weighed, fully loaded, 6.1 million pounds, thirteen times as much as the Statue of Liberty. The first stage had five engines, each nineteen feet tall, and contained nearly five million pounds of fuel, liquid oxygen and refined kerosene, which it burned in 150 seconds, producing 160 million horsepower or 7.5 million pounds of thrust. (The V-2's engine had delivered a thrust of 50,000 pounds.) The noise of the five engines was sufficient to suggest to one witness, Norman Mailer, that at last "man now had something with which to speak to God."[18] The *Saturn V* was and may remain forever the most awesome of the glamour projectiles.

On July 20, 1969, the thrust of the first-stage engines lifted all three of the *Saturn's* stages to an altitude of forty-one miles and a speed of 5,400 miles per hour. As the first stage fell away, the second-stage engine, with over a million pounds of fuel, liquid oxygen and liquid hydrogen, fired, increasing the speed to more than 15,000 miles per hour. At an altitude of 120 miles it jettisoned and the third-stage engine ignited briefly, again fueled with liquid oxygen and hydrogen, increasing the speed to 17,000 miles per hour, inserting the craft in an orbit around Earth. When the craft was in the right position in relation to the Moon to swerve out of orbit and depart for that goal, the astronauts reignited the single engine, thrusting their vehicle to 190 miles in altitude and a speed of

---

[17] Frank H. Winter, *Rockets into Space* (Cambridge: Harvard University Press, 1990), 81.
[18] Norman Mailer, *Of a Fire on the Moon* (Boston: Little, Brown and Co., 1970), 100.

24,300 miles per hour, escape velocity. Then they coasted to the orbit of the Moon, where no human, no organism, nothing with the pretension of a single strand of DNA, had ever existed before.[19]

On July 20, 1969, Neil Armstrong and Edwin Aldrin descended a ladder from the spacecraft that had ridden aloft in the tip of a *Saturn V* and stepped down on to the surface of the Moon. Tsiokovsky, Goddard, Oberth (the latter, miraculously, was present at Cape Kennedy for the launch, as he had been for the first successful launch of the V-2 at Peenemünde) were vindicated. This was a day of triumph for their theories and vision, and for American techno-scientific ingenuity, industrial might, and its catch-as-catch-can immigration policy in 1945.

One of the best of the "prisoners of peace," Arthur Rudolph, had been project leader specifically responsible for the creation of the *Saturn V*.[20] For his services to the United States he was received by presidents and awarded the Exceptional Civilian Service Award by the U.S. Army and the Exceptional Service Medal and Distinguished Service Medal by NASA. On the occasion of his retirement, Representative Robert Jones placed a tribute to him into the *Congressional Record:* "I commend him on his outstanding achievements in our Nation's missile and space programs, and I wish Dr. Rudolph and his family every happiness in their future years."

When information on Rudolph's service as production engineer for the V-2 at Mittelwerk and his possible complicity in atrocities there emerged in 1982, he gave up his American citizenship and returned to Germany, where he died, an exile in the land of his

---

[19] Winter, *Rockets into Space,* 83–5; John Duncan, "The Saturn V," http://www.apollosaturn.com.

[20] See Wegener, *The Peenemünde Wind Tunnel: A Memoir* (New Haven, CT: Yale University Press, 1966), (New Hv 140, 152–5; "National Archives to Open Heinrich Mueller and Arthur Rudolph Files (Record Group 319), National Archives and Records Administration, http://www.nara.gov/iwg/declass/rg319html.

birth.[21] Wernher von Braun, his good reputation intact, had died five years earlier in Alexandria, Virginia.

The story of space rocketry since the first Moon walk has been a matter of practical triumphs and cosmic frustrations. The near heavens are full of satellites delivering blizzards of phone calls and e-mails, producing data for better maps and weather prediction, checking for pollution, spying on potential enemies, keeping watch for outbursts of solar radiation, peering into the depths of the universe and its past, and so on. Space stations whirl around our planet. Space shuttles ascend like rockets and descend and land like airplanes.

But what we might call the heroic era of space exploration seems to be over or at least on hold. Von Braun pronounced the Moon landing "equal in importance to the moment in evolution when aquatic life came crawling up on land."[22] Few in power shared his enthusiasm. In December 1972 the last of the twelve humans who have visited the Moon returned home. There has been since no implementation of plans for permanent bases there, and nothing more than preliminary studies for manned trips to Mars. We are, to follow along with von Braun's analogy, still on the beach.

The fear that drove governments to spend money by the truck-load for the initial ventures into space dissipated. In the 1970s the Soviet Union was in decline and with it rocket rivalry for world leadership. In time the Americans and Russians would be offering each other and others hospitality in their space vehicles and

---

[21] Wegener, *The Peenemünde Wind Tunnel*, 152–5; Thomas Franklin, *An American in Exile: The Story of Arthur Rudolph* (Huntsville, AL: Christopher Kayor Co., 1983), 122, 126, 137, 145. "National Archives to Open Heinrich Mueller and Arthur Randolph Files" (Record Group 319), National Archives and Records Administration, http://www.nara.gov/iwg/declass/rg319html.

[22] Mailer, *Of a Fire on the Moon*, 72–3.

stations. Nostalgia for balanced budgets damped the wild nationalism and technological romanticism of the Americans in the 1950s and 1960s.

Where the zealots for deep space exploration were once grandiose, they now had to be shrewd. Their funds shrank, but the weight they saved by instrument miniaturization and by omitting lunky astronauts from the payload compensated for some of that. The best example of the trend toward frugality and technological restraint was a space vehicle called *Pioneer 10,* which was already on its way to Jupiter when the last human walked on the surface of the Moon.[23]

Pioneer 10 was – *is* (we must speak of it, no matter how unimaginably remote it is, in the present tense) – a 570-pound, plutonium powered epitome of the split personality of the space program. Its makers, scientists and engineers, loaded it with instruments to gather data about interplanetary environment – dust, cosmic rays, magnetic fields, solar wind – and about Jupiter, the biggest and, by most standards, the least worldly of planets.

Its makers, among them Carl Sagan, a scientist trying to succeed von Braun as a publicist, fastened a gold-anodized aluminum plaque to its side for the edification, supposedly, of extraterrestrials (really for the popular press). Incised into the metal are symbols representing, among other things, the number 8 in binary form, the path through space planned for this space probe, the position of our Sun relative to nearby pulsars, and depictions of a woman and man. The woman is doing nothing. The man is holding up his right forelimb in what NASA hoped, in a supernova burst of optimism, that extraterrestrials would recognize as the universal signal

---

[23] Frank White, *The Overview Effect: Space Exploration and Human Evolution,* 2nd ed. (Reston, VA: American Institute of Aeronautics and Astronautics, 1998), 37.

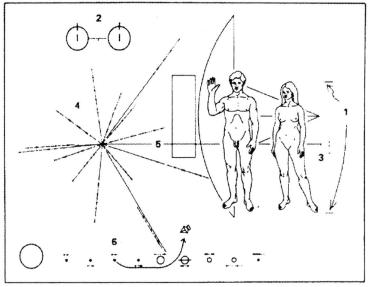

Figure 14. The *Pioneer 10* plaque, with indications for the edification of extragalaxtic species of the location of our solar system and the earth therein and a great deal more. Also included are sketches of two human beings, one with a hand raised in a just possibly universal gesture of good-will. NASA.

of peace. With this plaque NASA deftly trivialized the awesome (Fig. 14).[24]

The reaction to the plaque at the time of the space probe's launch was mixed. Many were amused. Feminists were offended by the woman's passivity. Prudes sputtered that the human couple was naked and that NASA was sending smut into space. The Chicago *Sun-Times* erased the man's genitals and the woman's breasts before printing a picture of the plaque.[25]

[24] http://spaceprojects.arc.nasa.gov/; http://quest.arc.nasa.gov/pioneer10/mission/.
[25] Burrows, *This New Ocean,* 483.

Pioneer 10 failed as a billboard, but has been gloriously successful as what it is, a space probe. It blasted off on top of an Atlas/Centaur/TE364-4 rocket on March 2, 1972. The first stage produced over 400,000 pounds of thrust, the Centaur and second stage 29,000 pounds, and the TE364-4 and third stage 15,000 pounds. When the third stage burned out, the Pioneer 10 was traveling at 32,000 miles (52,000 kilometers) per hour, faster than any object yet made by humans. It passed the Moon's orbit in eleven hours and Mars's in twelve weeks. In July it began its seven-month journey through the asteroid belt; it survived. As it neared Jupiter, the gravitational pull of the enormous planet accelerated the probe's speed to 82,000 miles (132,000 kilometers) an hour. It passed around the planet, collecting data on its mass, temperature, moons, radiation belts, temperature, thermal balance, atmosphere. At closest approach, on December 3, 1973, it was only 81,000 miles above the planet's cloud tops. It transmitted back to its creators their first "close-up" images of Jupiter, of its Great Red Spot, and then whiplashed around the planet and hurtled away from the Sun at a velocity fifty-five times that of a rifle bullet and off toward interstellar space.[26]

Little has happened to it since. In December 1992 it "experienced a gravitational deflection," that is, passed through the gravitational field of a considerable something, probably a remnant of our primordial solar nebula, at a distance from the Sun of fifty-six Astronomical Units. (An AU is the distance from the Earth to Sun, a standard unit for measuring astronomical lengths) (Fig. 15).

As of the beginning of the third millennium of the Common Era, *Pioneer 10* is as far from Earth as light travels in ten and a half

---

[26] http://spaceprojects.arc.nasa.gov/; Mark Wolverton, "The Spacecraft That Will Not Die," *American Heritage of Invention and Technology*, Vol. 3 (Winter 2001), 47–58.

Figure 15. *Pioneer 10* on its way to Aldebaran. NASA.

hours. The probe's speed, relative to the Sun, is 12.24 kilometers per second (27,380 miles per hour).[27] It still receives and answers to signals from Earth. This capability is not expected to last much longer.

Now sailing through the immaculate vacuum of interstellar space, *Pioneer 10* will in all probability continue on and arrive in

[27] http://spaceprojects.arc.nasa.gov/Space_Projects/pioneer/PNStat.html. Pioneer 10, by the way, is not the most distant of human-made objects. That is Voyager 1, launched September 5, 1977. As of January 2001, roundtrip light time from earth to Voyager 1 was over twenty-two hours.

the vicinity of Aldebaran, sixty-eight light years away, in about two million years. *Pioneer 10* will almost certainly outlast its home planet, which will be destroyed in five billion years when our Sun becomes a red giant.[28]

[28] http://spaceprojects.arc.nasa.gov/; http://quest.arc.nasa.gov/pioneer10/ mission.

The Fourth Acceleration

The Earth is the cradle of the mind, but we cannot live forever in a cradle.

Konstantine E. Tsiokovsky (1911)[1]

One of the hardest parts of working there was trying not to spend too much time looking back at the earth.

Jeffrey A. Hoffman (1985)[2]

The capability to effect changes at a distance helped our chimpish progenitors to survive on the African savannah; to procure more and better foods; eventually to migrate across the globe and adapt to varied environments; to extinguish whole divisions of life forms, perhaps including hominid species, certainly to eliminate many subdivisions within the *Homo*

[1] www:informatics.org/museum/tsiol.html.
[2] Frank White, *The Overview Effect: Space Exploration and Human Evolution*, 2nd ed. (Reston, VA: American Institute of Aeronauttics, 1998), 236.

sapiens species. Throwing and fire, moreover, may have helped us to think abstractly, to think about what is past and gone and what may yet come.

Projectile and fire technology has lifted us off the Earth's surface in aircraft and into space in rocket craft. The latter are breath-takingly expensive and all destinations in space as scientifically conceived at present are viciously inhospitable. Even so, the history of our genus and our species indicates that we will continue with our sorties aloft.

Throwing is as characteristic of our kind as running is of cheetahs. When Alan Shepard and Edgar Mitchell, the third pair of our species to walk on the Moon, finished their assigned tasks there in February 1971 they stole an opportunity to indulge an idle whim. The occasion was a Rorschach test of sorts. What would they do to mark in their memories this ineffable scene of two humans impossibly remote from oceans, grass, trees, birds, and children; what could they do to assert their humanity in the moon's soul-shriveling bleakness?

Shepard had smuggled golf balls and a six-iron club head into space with him. He attached the head to the handle of a rock collector stick and hit a ball which soared, he proclaimed, "miles and miles and miles," that is to say, about fifty to sixty feet – not bad for a golfer whose pressure suit restricted him to a one-handed swing.

Mitchell took the staff from a piece of equipment called a Solar Wind Composition Collector, wound up as best he could in his pressure suit, and threw it like a spear. Shepard rated the effort as "the greatest javelin throw of the century," in other words about equal to his six-iron drive. An observer at Ground Control on Earth, watching the hominids having fun on television, judged Mitchell's heave as "actually a fairly credible throw. You took a big hop forward, right leg leading, and got your left arm moving forward reasonably well at shoulder height."[3]

A Schöningen javelinist 400,000 years ago would not have been wearing a space suit and would, therefore, have managed a direct overhand throw, but otherwise would have propelled his missile with a similar sequence of motions. It is how we hominids have thrown, throw now, and will throw in the future.

All extraterrestrial environments are, as far as we know, instantaneously fatal to unprotected human beings. We can exist "out there" only in sealed compartments (living quarters or suits) enclosing earthly environments, that is atmosphere with oxygen, temperatures that won't sear or freeze-dry our flesh, and so on. These compartments have to be carefully shielded against radiation, of which there is a seething abundance in space.

Even if these needs are answered, extra-earthly environments are and will differ drastically from those of the home planet. Hominids and all life as we know it have evolved under the influence of an unvarying pull of gravity. The Sun shines or does not, the wind blows soft or hard, even the ground may quake, but gravity, according to our bodily perceptions, is always the same. It will almost never be of steady earthly magnitude, off our planet. Gravity on the Moon is one-sixth of what we literally know

---

[3] Eric M. Jones, ed. "Apollo 14 Lunar Surface Journal, EVA-2 Close-out and Golf Shots," http://www.hq.nasa.gov/office/pao/History/alsj/a14/a14.clsout2.html, 35:08:17–35:21:33, Robert Godwin, *Apollo 14: The NASA Mission Reports* (Burlington, Ontario, Canada: Apogee Books, 2000), CDROM Apollo 14 Movies and Images, EDGAR29MPG, EDGAR30B.MPG. It should be noted that Mitchell, the first javelinist in space, returned to earth to found an Institute of Noetic Sciences and to become a combination scientist and philosopher-mystic. See Edgar Mitchell, *The Way of the Explorer* (New York: G. P. Putnam, 1996).

in our bones is right and proper. Humans who have "walked" on the Moon have found that skipping is the best means of locomotion there, a discovery that suggests that stranger discoveries are in store.[4]

We know a lot about what life will be like in unearthly gravities. We have learned about what happens to the human body during weeks and months of exposure to weightlessness or near weightlessness in orbiting space platforms. Bones and muscles, which no longer have to deal with weight, lose density and mass. Fluids surge to the chest and head because gravity no longer pulls them down into the legs. The legs shrink, spinal disks expand, the heart goes flabby, and red blood cell production drops. The body excretes what it interprets as extra fluid, along with essentials such as calcium, electrolytes, and blood plasma. David A. Wolf lost forty percent of his muscle mass, twelve percent of bone, and twenty-three pounds during four and a half months on board the Russian Mir.[5]

These may be challenges that we will be able to answer satisfactorily with exercise, calcium and vitamin supplements, and special equipment. There are other and more difficult problems, however. Space travelers, bereft of the defenses of the Earth's magnetic field and of its atmosphere, are naked unto solar and cosmic radiation. Storms on the Sun fire off sudden blasts of intense radiation. Fortunately, their dissemination through the solar system are not instantaneous and so space travelers, warned by their own monitors or from Earth, should have time to take shelter within radiation-proof hideaways within their spacecrafts.

---

[4] Alberto E. Minetti, "The Biomechanics of Skipping Gaits: A Third Locomotion Paradigm?" *Proceedings of the Royal Society of London, Biology*, Vol. 265 (1998), 1227.

[5] Michael E. Long, "Surviving in Space," *National Geographic*, Vol. 199 (January 2001), 20.

Cosmic rays, which are radiation from sources beyond the solar system, pose a more difficult problem. They provide no warning and pass right through shielding, on through the human body, disrupting atoms and molecules as they go.

We know little about the psychosocial problems of space flight, of months and years of soul-chilling remoteness from all that is familiar, of long isolation in tiny quarters with no possibility of real privacy and with the same few people. A trip to Mars would take about 260 days. Then there would be the excitement of actually being on that planet, but isolation in close quarters with the same comrades would continue. Then the voyage back to Earth, arriving at home after, shall we say, 600–700 days in a tin can with the same smelly, stupid people.

Mars is our next-door neighbor. Voyages to more distant destinations would take much longer. Settlements on one of Saturn's moons, would require some people to spend years, even lifetimes, away from their home planet. They might terraform as their ancestors did on their home planet. But what would it be like to live where our Sun would be no more comfort than a very bright star?[6]

Every given situation ultimately engenders its opposite, its antithesis. Projectile technology reinforces the human sense of specialness and separateness, and tempts us to think of ourselves as apart from the biosphere. It empowers us as the great re-arranger, even exterminator, perhaps even of other species of hominids. It encourages each of us to think of him or herself as a starkly separate entity. It encourages and enables some of us to impose our ways on others of our own species.

The antithesis would be that projectile technology in its recent manifestation as space travel would amplify our sense of

---

[6] Long, "Surviving in Space," 6–29; Ronald White and Maurice Ayerner, "Humans in Space," *Nature*, Vol. 409 (February 22, 2001), 1115–8.

kinship with the other organisms of the biosphere and, at the same time, encourage cultural diversity or even genetic diversity.

Dispersal through space to settlements whose remoteness from each other will be described in astronomical units or in hours of radio signal round trips will increase cultural diversity as migration did when we first spread out of Africa and around the world. As we live and reproduce in different worlds with different founding populations, different gravities, different microlife (either imported or, just possibly, local "extremophilic" species), different radiation regimens, different foods, and so on, we will inevitably evolve in new ways.[7] We may even resort to genetic engineering to hurry our adaptations. The *Homo sapiens* species will redifferentiate back into a normally multibranched genus. The hominid lineage, since the Pleistocene as single-trunked as a palm tree with us as the fronds and nuts on top, will revert to primordial bushiness.

In space, looking back at Earth and isolated from all earthly life except for what we've carted across the galaxy, we will rediscover reverence for that life. That empyrean change in attitude has already begun. For millions of us the iconic image of our era is not a picture of the detonation of an H-bomb but of the Earth as seen from the Moon. For the first time we observed the earthly biosphere, all species, all human groups, as a single entity. Materialists and mystics alike were awed.

British physicist and novelist C. P. Snow recoiled from the Moon. The solar system "is dead, apart from our world ... We can explore a few lumps in our system, and that is the end..." The distance to the stars makes further human exploration

---

[7] Hints about this can be found in Alberto E. Minetti, "Biomechanics: Walking on Other Planets," *Nature*, Vol. 409 (January 25, 2001), 467–9.; White and Ayerner, "Humans in Space," 1115–8.

Figure 16. Earthrise from lunar orbit. NASA.

beyond impossible. "As a result of supreme technological skill and heroism, we are faced not with the infinite but with the immovable limits."[8]

The Moon set physician and essayist Thomas Lewis to musing about his own celestial home. "Viewed from the distance of the moon, the astonishing thing about the earth, catching the breath, is that it is alive (Fig. 16). The photographs show the dry, pounded surface of the moon in the foreground, dead as an old bone. [Deader, actually. The bone was alive once.] Aloft, floating free

[8] C. P. Snow, "The Moon Landing," *Look*, XXXIII (August 26, 1969), 72.

beneath the moist, gleaming membrane of bright, blue sky, is the rising earth, the only exuberant thing in this part of the cosmos."[9]

In the 1960s the National Aeronautics and Space Administration of the United States commissioned the biologist and atmosphere scientist, James E. Lovelock, to join in the investigation of the possibility of life on Mars. His inquiry left him doubting that possibility and in awe of its plenitude on Earth, where conditions not just permit but stimulate life in myriad variety and propagations.

He knew that the Earth's siblings, Venus and Mars, are planets of temperature extremes, boiling and frozen hells, respectively. Their atmospheres are almost entirely composed of carbon dioxide, poisonous to animal life as we know it, and with oxygen, essential to animal life, in tiny amounts. The Earth's temperature is moderate and narrow in variation, obviously suitable for life, and its air includes only slight amounts of carbon dioxide and twenty-one percent oxygen.

The moderation of earthly conditions intrigued him. If the oxygen amounted to less than twelve percent of its atmosphere, fire would be impossible. If over twenty-five percent, every fire would rage until every bit of combustible matter was consumed. There would be no campfires, only conflagrations, and soon none of those because there would be nothing left to burn.[10]

The Earth's air is "so curious and incompatible a mixture," Lovelock reasoned, "that it cannot possibly have arisen or persisted by chance." He proposed what has come to be known as the Gaia Hypothesis, named after the ancient Greek earth goddess. The hypothesis, in his words, supposes that "the atmosphere, the oceans, the climate, and the crust of the Earth

---

[9] Thomas Lewis, *The Lives of a Cell: Notes of a Biology Watcher* (New York: Viking Press, 1974), 145.

[10] J. E. Lovelock, *Gaia: A New Look at Life on Earth* (Oxford: Oxford University Press, 1987), 1, 36–39.

are regulated at a state comfortable for life because of the behavior of living organisms."[11]

He cites scientific data, not scripture, in support of his theory. The most persuasive bit of evidence for a lay audience is that we have air with oxygen in plenty only because of eons upon eons of the labor of cells with green chloroplasts which utilize sunlight to convert carbon dioxide and water to oxygen. We animals inhale it and, in our turn, exhale carbon dioxide, essential to plants.[12] The balance of oxygen and carbon dioxide is maintained by the utterly inattentive cooperation of the billions upon billions of organisms dependent upon that balance.

Gaia's validity is nothing we can decide here – many scientists condemn it as mysticism decked out in data – but it has meaning for us as a cultural artifact of our age and, as well, is significance as a monument of irony. Projectile technology, which began with our throwing rocks at fellow creatures, has led us to a recognition of the interdependence and wholeness and mutual supportiveness of life on Earth.

An even greater irony may await us. Projectile technology, which provides us with the means for our extinction, also provides us an avenue to immortality. If we use it to migrate to other bodies of our solar system, we will free ourselves and the life forms we take abroad with us from being hostages to the fate of one planet. When a comet next hits Earth, some of our clan may be watching from elsewhere in the solar system. Before our Sun explodes, we may be off in pursuit of *Pioneer 10*. Throwing might enable us to last as long as the universe.

[11] J. E. Lovelock, *The Ages of Gaia: A Biography of Our Living Earth* (New York: W. W. Norton, 1988), 19.
[12] Lovelock, *Ages of Gaia*, 127.

Index